floors

floors

A design source book

Elizabeth Wilhide *with photography by* **Henry Bourne**

STEWART, TABORI & CHANG
NEW YORK

First published in Great Britain in 1997 by
Ryland Peters & Small,
Cavendish House, 51-55 Mortimer Street,
London W1N 7TD

Published in 1997 and distributed by
Stewart, Tabori & Chang,
a division of U.S. Media Holdings, Inc.
115 West 18th Street, New York, New York 10011

Distributed in Canada by
General Publishing Ltd.
30 Lesmill Road
Don Mills, Ontario, M3B 2T6, Canada

Library of Congress Cataloging-in-Publication Data
Wilhide, Elizabeth.
    Floors / by Elizabeth Wilhide ; photography by Henry Bourne.
        p. cm. – (A design source book)
    Includes index.
    ISBN 1-55670-605-7 (hardcover)
    1. Flooring. 2. Floors–Design and construction. 3. Interior
decoration. I. Title. II. Series.
TH2521.256   1977   97–12778
721.6–dc21

Printed in Hong Kong
10 9 8 7 6 5 4 3 2 1
Produced by Sun Fung Offset Binding Company Limited

Contents

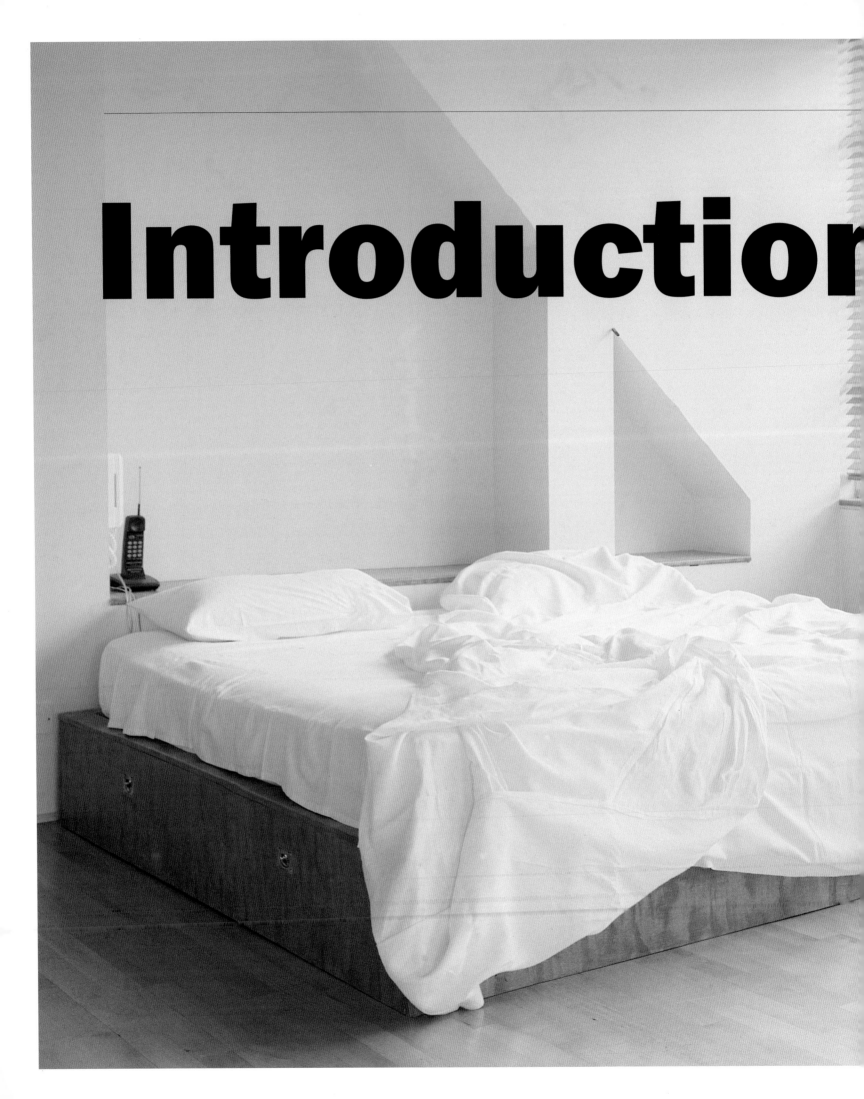

Introduction

The floor is a key element of the interior, literally the basis of every room. After walls and ceilings, floors represent the largest surface area in the home, which means that new flooring can entail a substantial investment of time, money, and effort, so it is especially important to get it right.

Equally important, the floor is a surface with which we are in more or less constant physical contact. Depending on its context, a floor may need to be comfortable, warm, quiet, safe, durable, easy to maintain, or meet any of a number of other physical requirements. At the same time, what the floor looks like — its basic character,

color, pattern, or texture — will inevitably set the tone for a decorating scheme. Technically, floors may be part of the background, but very few other elements of the interior have the potential to create such an impact on the way we live.

While it is easy to stand back and admire fresh paintwork or a new sofa, what goes on underfoot often escapes our attention. Yet a beautiful floor can do more for a room than almost any other aspect of decoration or furnishing. If you take the time and trouble to get the flooring right in your home, the rest will fall into place much more readily.

Choosing the right flooring is a decision that cannot be taken lightly — by and large, mistakes cannot be simply glossed over or hidden away. Before you begin to research alternatives, consider how all the areas in your home relate to one another. Ideally, flooring should be planned and chosen for the entire home rather than for one particular area at a time. If that is impossible, it is still important to choose flooring for one room with reference to what already exists or what is planned in other areas. This is not just to make sure there are no awkward clashes where one floor meets the next, but that the entire experience of moving through from one area to another is a natural and enjoyable progression.

Far left, above: An antique tiled floor, with rich pictorial motifs, lends architectural distinction to a period room.

Far left, below: Blond hardwood is a classic contemporary floor, combined here with glossy black resin.

Far left, center: Concrete need not be brutal. This matte-textured concrete floor has the look of brushed suede.

Left: Bold kilims define distinct areas in an open-plan space.

Above: Even humble materials such as plywood can have a stylish modern edge.

Top: Zigzagging ceramic tiles turn a staircase into graphic art.

Material quality

We tend to think of color, pattern, and texture as separate elements of design. To some extent this makes sense, particularly in the context of decoration, for example, where one aspect may well dominate the others. A red wall, for instance, may look subtly different with a flat or sheen paint finish, but there is no disguising the fact that the color is the key issue.

That distinction of separate design elements cannot apply to floors. There are, of course, certain situations where a splash of color or a bold pattern is exactly what is called for. But choice of flooring chiefly concerns materials and their intrinsic qualities. The color of a hardwood floor may be one of its attractions, but most people do not choose a wooden floor on the basis of its color alone. They make their selection after considering a number of related characteristics: the texture of the grain, the pattern of the boards, or the way the floor feels and sounds underfoot. Success with flooring often depends on an awareness of the way in which the elements work together to create a sense of character and style.

There is no escaping the fact that many of the flooring materials we find most beautiful and evocative do not come cheap, frequently because they derive from natural, often limited, sources. Natural materials add a fourth dimension to color, pattern, and texture — that of time. By and large, natural materials wear and age well, and many look better and better as the years go by. The same cannot be said of most synthetics; either the material is relatively impervious to change, which gives it a lifeless, static quality, or it degrades and looks tawdry as it wears.

This is not to argue against the use of artificial flooring in every circumstance. Synthetics have a number of persuasive practical advantages, the most eloquent being economy. Many artificial materials have been deliberately designed to give the appearance of their more expensive natural counterparts, but they cost far less. Saving labor is another important criterion, and many types of synthetic flooring are simpler to install and easier to maintain than natural materials. On stylistic grounds alone, however, synthetic flooring generally works best where it is a positive choice, rather than an obvious stand-in for something better.

Basically, it is a question of integrity. There is a vast difference between sheet vinyl that has been patterned and embossed to resemble brick and the same material in a simple checkerboard design. The latter may well suggest the effect of a black-and-white marble floor, but it is not setting out to deceive you.

In this context, lateral thinking can take you farther than simply substituting a down market simulation for the real thing. For many high-price solutions, there are more affordable alternatives that

Above: A concrete floor painted to match the walls envelops a room in saturated color.

Above right: Wide panels or planks have an expansive look, used to great effect in large spaces. This spruce floor has been simply sanded and sealed to reveal the grain of the wood.

Left: Mixing materials underfoot brings variety and character to the interior. Here the tiny grid of blue mosaic in the bathroom area makes an effective contrast with the main expanse of stripped floorboards.

Right: New, and sometimes surprising, flooring materials are emerging onto the market all the time. This graphic-looking area rug is made from woven paper twine.

can work surprisingly well. So if your heart is set on marble for the hall, but your bank balance won't bear the burden, try to identify which of the particular qualities of marble you find most attractive. If it is the smoothness and coolness of the stone, ceramic tile may provide a suitable alternative. If it is the association with period grandeur, marbleized floorboards might be the answer. If it is the sheer luxury of the material that appeals, you could either run a narrow border of marble tiles around a plain tiled floor or have them inset as threshold strips to give an elegant lift to more everyday surroundings.

When selecting flooring materials, bear in mind that patterns, colors, and textures can look very different under different lighting conditions and at different scales. Tiny samples or catalog pictures can be very misleading — as can showroom lighting.

Architectural character

Different materials also arouse specific responses as a result of their history of use in the interior. Subconsciously or not, this heritage aspect often influences our choices. Over the centuries, floors and floor coverings have been made from a vast range of materials, from mosaic to matting, from painted oilcloth to rammed earth. Ideas that seem fresh and original today often turn out to have quite a respectable pedigree. Natural-fiber coverings, for example, the style insider's choice since the mid-'80s, have their origins in the layers of rush that were strewn on the floors of English medieval hall houses, while King George IV appreciated the effect of richly decorated staterooms complemented by the simplicity of coir matting as long ago as the turn of the 19th century. And mosaic has been used since the time of the ancients.

The Renaissance marked an appreciable shift in attitudes to the interior and its design. Classical systems of design and decoration, which had originated in the ancient civilizations of Greece and Rome, were rediscovered and adopted wholesale by architects, artists, and craftsmen, first in Italy. This influence gradually spread, reaching the northern parts of Europe by the 18th century and then the New World, too.

A central tenet of the classical style was the notion of conceiving architectural space, its decoration and furnishing, as a single, unified scheme of design, rather than a series of distinct elements. In the homes and palaces of the very wealthy, imported marble and other decorative stone began to make an appearance as flooring materials, often fashioned into exquisite patterns, while in the

Nevertheless, in the majority of households up until the beginning of the industrialization age floors tended to be fairly basic and rudimentary. Buildings were largely fashioned from whatever materials were locally available — from stone quarried in the region and oak or other wood from nearby forests. And with very few exceptions, the floor was principally a structural element, nothing more, and carpets, which were rare and expensive items from the Orient or Near East, were prized treasures to be hung on walls or draped over tables.

grander houses wood flooring often took the form of geometric inlay known as marquetry or parquet. The floor began to be considered and designed in sympathy with other architectural features — mirroring the intricacies of a classical ceiling, for example, was one device that became the hallmark of the English architect Robert Adam.

With the establishment of carpet making at Wilton and Axminster in south western England and the court manufactures in France, carpet became more readily available and began to be used on the floor rather than displayed as a wall hanging. But for the majority, however, carpeted floors remained a luxury. In Britain, the elegance and refinement of the Georgian interior was more commonly complemented by relatively unfinished wooden floors

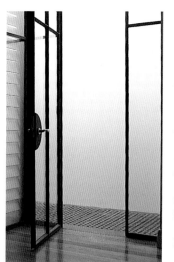

Far left: Pale hardwood strip marries well with the light, airy structure of a conservatory.

Center left: Broken limestone flags have a rustic look.

Far left: A pristine oak floor gives a lift to period paneling.

Below left: A modern art rug adds a soft layer in a minimal interior.

Below: Cool, stylish terrazzo is ideal for hot climates.

Left: Decking and hardwood.

laid in boards, cleaned with sand, the light tone of the wood marrying well with the cool, pale colors that are characteristic of 18th-century decoration. The same type of simplicity is evident in classic Scandinavian interiors of the period, and in American Colonial and Federal houses, where the boards tended to be wider and were sometimes painted or decorated with simple motifs or stenciled patterns. Rag, hooked, or braided rugs, flat-weave "ingrain" carpet, and painted floorcloths were more usual coverings than fine carpet.

With the progress of industrialization, however, carpet became more affordable and widely available. New synthetic pigments and dyes were developed, and in Britain the Victorian love of ornament and pattern was displayed in vividly colored and richly detailed carpets. These were often laid wall to wall, or with only a small margin of exposed wooden floor, usually stained a dark color to blend with the rest of the woodwork. Alternatively, the margin might be filled by a utilitarian covering such as drugget, oilcloth, or linen. A wool rug or animal skin took pride of place in front of the hearth.

Above: A traditional pattern of octagonal tiles inset with keystones, has been given a contemporary twist. Restricting the number of dark keystones reduces the insistence of the design and makes it fresher-looking.

Right: Simple, integral flooring, such as this hardwood strip, keeps the attention focused on the organic shapes and bright colors of the furniture. The reflective sheen of the flooring maximizes the effect of natural light spilling through the venetian blinds. A softer, more light-absorbent floor covering, such as wall-to-wall carpeting, would have produced a much less lively and spacious feeling.

On ground floors, in halls, and in utility rooms, where floors had always been made of heavy, durable materials such as fired earth, stone, and brick, new materials began to be used. Encaustic tiles, with their Gothic motifs, expressed the 19th-century fascination with medieval art and were a popular treatment for hallways and porches in Britain from the midcentury on. Oilcloth was a similarly serviceable and cheap alternative, often exuberantly decorated in simulation of other more expensive materials. Its successor, linoleum, appeared around the turn of the century.

The introduction of linoleum coincided with a new concern to create more hygienic surroundings, where dust and vermin could not lurk in heavy drapery or carpeted floors. This desire for a clean sweep meant that wall-to-wall carpeting was replaced by smaller rugs laid over polished or stained boards which were easier to

maintain. Gradually, as the century turned, the trend was toward more lightness in the interior: parquet and woodblock flooring became fashionable; and, particularly under the influence of the Arts and Crafts movement, quarry tiles and brick became more commonplace.

Throughout the 20th century, the choice of synthetic floors has increased at a great rate, while natural flooring materials from all over the world have also become more widely available. Simultaneously, a wealth of stylistic influences has come into play – influences as diverse as the Mediterranean villa and the traditional Japanese house, the Cornish cottage and the Manhattan loft, and even, in the industrial aesthetic of high-tech, the factory or commercial office. It is perfectly possible to create any style that takes your fancy. Given this breadth of choice, it can often be difficult to know where to begin.

Below: Concrete has emerged as a stylish flooring material for contemporary interiors, finally shrugging off its old image of ugly, gray utility. These concrete panels, colored to a deep terracotta, have a raw earthy quality that suits the elemental setting.

Below right: Carpeting inset among wooden borders suggest the traditional modular format of tatami matting in Japanese houses.

Bottom right: A harmonious combination of time-honored flooring materials makes a sympathetic solution for a period house. Black and white marble tiles in the entrance hall contrast with herringbone parquet and a bordered carpet in the living room. The original stone staircase is also carpeted to provide a welcome degree of comfort and sound insulation.

Victorian encaustic tiles hiding their glory under the cracked linoleum in the hall of an older house, it is far from uncommon to find relatively intact original floors buried under more utilitarian coverings. Brought to light, refinished, and with any missing elements replaced, such floors contribute a unique and satisfying sense of character that more than offsets the time and effort spent on their restoration.

But you don't have to live in the country to relish rugged materials and natural colors or nubbly textures — and neither do you need to own a fine period property to enjoy old flagstones or hardwood parquet. If you have an overall sense of your own tastes and what you are trying to achieve, the result will inevitably have greater vitality than following stylistic blueprints to the letter.

One useful starting point when it comes to creating a sense of style is to consider the period and architectural character of your home. Of course, there is no law that says you must preserve original features and forms of decoration right down to the last doorknob or fingerplate, but a basic sympathy for context can help guide your choices. And although a floor covering is a renewable, superficial treatment, the floor itself is literally built into the fabric and structure of the house, so respecting or restoring what is already there is often the most successful approach to adopt if your home displays any degree of architectural merit or distinction that is worth keeping.

The growing interest in period styles and historic interiors means that it is now easier than ever before to find the information you need and to source the materials necessary for restoring or replacing an original floor. While not everyone is going to discover

Scale and proportion

Most of us would like to live in more spacious surroundings than those we already inhabit. But you don't have to physically enlarge your home to increase the feeling of space within it. The right choice of flooring is one important way in which you can create a sense of openness and expansion.

In very small apartments or houses, the most straightforward approach may be to run the same flooring more or less throughout. This has a unifying effect where space is cramped and provides a basic simplicity that helps to counteract lack of scale. In small homes, a significantly greater proportion of space is often taken up by circulation areas such as halls, landings, and stairs, which means that you are more aware of the transitions from room to room and area to area. Running the same flooring throughout helps to lessen the impact of these transitions simply because you draw less attention to them.

The obvious risk with such an approach is blandness. But whereas yards of neutral-toned carpet would undoubtedly be boring and uninspiring, there are many livelier alternatives that can still enhance spatial quality without looking dull. The secret is to opt for flooring materials that have their own innate sense of liveliness or interest. In such situations, natural fiber coverings such as sisal, jute, or coir, are much more appealing than cut pile carpet because the nubbliness of the weave and texture of the fibers provides an added dimension.

It is rarely possible to extend the same flooring into absolutely every corner of the home. Hardworking areas such as kitchens and bathrooms tend to need more practical floors than those designed for general living spaces. Nevertheless, the quality of space will not be undermined if you keep to the same tonal range when flooring these areas. Linoleum, vinyl, and ceramic tile now come in such a wide variety of colors that making a good match with the main flooring is not difficult.

In open-plan spaces, multipurpose rooms, or where there is more than one level, diversity rather than unity may be what is required. Here, the choice of flooring can help to define different areas of use and break up the monotony of a large surface.

Practicalities aside, large open areas can look rather amorphous without some sense of definition to humanize the scale. To take an extreme example, a loft or converted warehouse is potentially among the most exciting of all living spaces. But for the space to be exhilarating rather than intimidating, it has to be treated as a series of related areas rather than one vast stage set with furniture and fixtures which can look marooned in isolated groups. So wherever you want to retain the sense of openness

Left: Textural contrast makes an important contribution in interiors where backgrounds must remain in the background. Here loose-laid sisal matting, with its coarse, nubbly weave, is a perfect complement to the bleached, distressed surface of reclaimed oak boards. Where flooring materials are used in combination, detailing is crucial. The neat jute edge binding on the sisal matting both prevents fraying and makes the effect look well considered.

Below: In minimal interiors, simplicity can be deceiving, demanding a high degree of perfection in execution and finish. Where the wide planks of hardwood flooring meet the plane of the wall, the wall is carried over on an inset beading instead of being finished with more traditional baseboards. The effect is to "float" the walls over the floor and accentuate the pure sculptural quality of the architecture.

without inducing a feeling of agoraphobia, using different flooring materials in different areas introduces a suggestion of enclosure that will make the space easier to live in.

Other factors have an impact on our perceptions of scale and proportion. As in all aspects of decoration, pale or neutral tones increase the impression of light and space, whereas darker shades provide a greater sense of warmth and enclosure. In a similar way, the reflective sheen of harder materials, say, polished wood or tile, can enhance a feeling of spaciousness, while matte surfaces, such as pile carpet, which are light absorbent, have the opposite effect.

The way you lay flooring that is composed of repetitive elements, such as boards or tile, also has a bearing. Strips of hardwood laid parallel to the length of a room lead the eye onward. Herringbone patterns made with brick, wood block, or parquet are more dynamic than basketweave designs, because they introduce a sense of direction and forward movement. Using tiles of a scale to suit the space in which they are laid is important. A widely spaced grid of big tiles or blocks looks expansive in a large area; in a small room, large tiling only calls attention to the lack of floor area.

But all rules are made to be broken. In a small confined space, the answer may be to acknowledge the limitation of scale and play up to it with jewel-bright color or geometric patterning. Strong color is uplifting, but you can have too much of a good thing, and what works in relatively small doses may well be exhausting or simply too dominant in large measure.

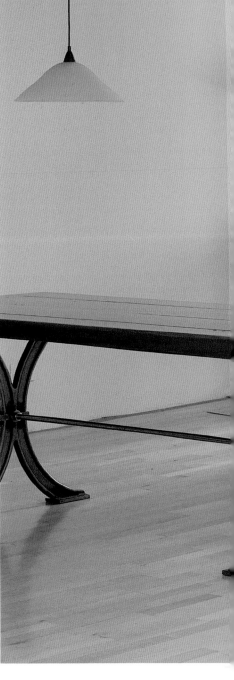

Top left: Cool limestone has a monumental quality paired with luminous blue wall tiles.

Top right: A modern take on Moorish style has a terrazzo floor inlaid with colorful fragments.

Opposite above left: Pale French limestone flooring is extended from the main living space right out into the garden terrace to dissolve the boundaries between indoors and out. In situations where you cannot extend precisely the same flooring material into outdoor areas, an equivalent effect can be achieved either by choosing a more durable material from the same family, such as stone or wood, or by choosing a material of a similar color or texture.

Opposite left: Here a dynamic, directional effect has been achieved by insetting an arrowhead of stone tile within the expanse of hardwood floor, with the apex lined up to lead the eye to the adjoining landing and staircase.

Above: In open-plan spaces, the challenge is to retain the feeling of spaciousness while defining distinct areas, a task achieved here by flooring the kitchen area in rubber to contrast with hardwood elsewhere.

Connections and combinations

Outdoors we tend to be acutely aware of changes in terrain. Part of the pleasure of a country walk is the way different textures and surfaces are encountered underfoot. The scrunch of gravel, the springiness of grass, the soft rustle of leaves in the woods all contribute to the experience. Conversely, we tire quickly of walking in urban areas if the surface is unremitting asphalt or concrete.

The same basic enjoyment of surface can be provided when you make your choice of flooring for the home. Sometimes, especially where space is very cramped, it is necessary to keep to the same flooring throughout the home; but in most cases, a combination of different materials helps keep the space alive. Varying the type of floor from area to area does not imply that you have to assault the eye with clashing colors and patterns or make abrupt changes of style. It simply means being aware of the way in which changes of surface or texture can add vitality and interest, a subtle shift in gear from one room to the next.

In an open-plan area, one of the simplest and most straightforward ways to achieve the required distinction is with a rug or series of rugs. In a large room, a rug will help to draw a seating arrangement together; in a combined living/dining space, a rug under the table and chairs will add a touch of formality and graciousness. It is important to choose the right size rug for the scale of the room. Small rugs scattered around a big space will only look lost.

A further dimension can be achieved by varying the flooring material. There are often good practical reasons for combining different types of floor in the same space. In a kitchen/dining room or where a kitchen is included within the main living area, a robust and easily maintained floor is usually the best option for the hardworking part of the room — the cooking and food-preparation area — while a softer floor may be preferred in the rest of the space.

With this approach, it makes sense to find a natural break. The dividing line can be determined by the architecture or structure of the room or by the way the space is used. Where two rooms have been knocked together, the position of the former wall is a good place to change from one type of floor to another, particularly if there is an archway or a margin of retaining wall on each side of the opening. If a kitchen has been built into one end of a living room, behind a counter or half-height divider, the most obvious solution would be to run the main flooring up to the counter and treat the kitchen floor differently.

The most discreet way of combining floors in open-plan areas is to vary the material without varying the tone. A light hardwood floor in a dining area would make a seamless partner to light ceramic tile in the kitchen end of the room, for example.

Top: Material mix can be as simple and straightforward as a scatter rug over reclaimed floorboards.

Above: Echoing the combination of materials in kitchen units and shelving, metal kitchen flooring meets wooden floorboards.

Left: Subtle variety of textures underfoot: wood meets concrete inset with a generously scaled coir mat.

Top right: Here stainless-steel sheet flooring is combined with siliceous pebbles set in resin for an unusual textural contrast.

Above right: Slate laid in staggered rows gives onto the airy expanse of maple floorboards.

Right: Strong contrasts can be equally as effective as sympathetic matches. Here brick paviors are crisply offset by a border of white marble, an economical way of using an expensive material.

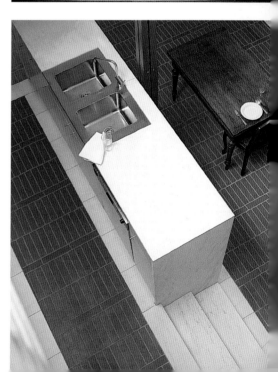

Left: A study in elegant contrast is provided by this unusual flooring combination, a panel of recycled "ironbark" timber (an Australian hardwood) is set within saturnia stone, which is a type of unfilled travertine.

Right: An excellent way of marking the boundary between indoors and out is achieved with a change of surface underfoot: here warm, tactile wood flooring meets stone paving.

But it can be equally effective to make a bolder contrast of material, color, or pattern. Where there is no natural break, or the way you use the space does not conform to a structural division, you can use flooring in a freer way to provide a sense of definition. This often works best where you retain the same flooring material throughout but vary the color or pattern. Sheet linoleum is a good material for this type of treatment: you can use curving contours of contrasting color to signal the change from one area to the next. A cheap and effective way of defining areas is to paint or stencil a border on floorboards to create a space within a space or introduce a patterned tiled floor within a greater expanse of plain tiling. On the whole, however, bold contrasts do not work well with carpet. It is nearly always better to avoid any situation where carpets of differing colors, textures, or patterns meet without some intermediary shift to a different material.

Changing levels similarly provide a good excuse to vary floor treatments; in fact, a change of level that is not marked out in this way can look distinctly awkward in certain circumstances. Then there is the safety aspect to consider. Where part of a room is

Right: Where there are views through a sequence of rooms, different floor treatments provide visual interest and a sense of character. Here herringbone parquet flooring is separated from traditional floorboards by the black-and-white marble of the tiled hallway.

Center right: Tonally very similar, sisal in the hallway meets herringbone parquet. Metal edging between the two materials gives a neat finish.

Far right: A provocative material mix is shown in this combination of purple tasseled rug and textured rubber flooring.

Left (and detail, right): Changes of level provide the ideal opportunity to shift from one flooring material to another. Here an open metal staircase descends to a plinth of stone, which steps down to the main beechwood flooring.

Center right: The practical quarry-tiled kitchen floor makes a sympathetic match with hardwood and a flat-weave runner.

Far right: Textural contrast is supplied by a bubble-weave rug over slate.

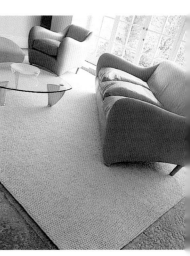

Above: Nothing is more theatrical than glass flooring. These superbly detailed glass stairs have an unbeatable sense of drama.

Above: The mellow tones of a brick floor complement the painted brick walls. A flat-weave cotton rug provides definition for a dining area.

either a step up or down from the remainder of the space, you can emphasize the transition with a change of flooring material and reduce the risk of someone missing a step.

Stairways indicate another change of pace and offer a logical place to switch from one type of material to another. The theatrical sweep of a staircase descending into a hall can be emphasized by just this sort of contrast, but even a modest flight of stairs looks good in a different finish.

Another trick is to combine materials over the same floor area. This is an excellent way to create textural variety, and it can also provide an economical yet effective means of using a more expensive material in smaller quantities. There are certain classic, complementary combinations, from the traditional white marble with inset diamonds of black slate to the more cozy partnerships of brick or terra-cotta and wood, but whatever materials you put together should show some basic affinity, either in terms of style or character.

Floor-level detail

Most floors occupy a relatively large surface area, but that does not mean you can afford to overlook the details. No matter how beautiful a floor may be, the full effect can be severely undermined by paying insufficient attention to what at first may appear relatively insignificant elements — such as junctions or edges, which should always look considered and neat. Finished edges not only look better, they perform better, too. Unprotected edges are more likely to fray and degrade and may even trip you up. Certain materials can be successfully butted up against each other, provided they are of similar thickness, but it is usual to cover the seam with a strip. Aluminum or brass cover strips are the standard means of finishing the edge of carpeting, particularly where it meets a new material. If you are running a carpet through several rooms, however, a seamed junction in the doorways would be less obtrusive. Beveled wooden strips can be run at the edge of hardwood floors or in thresholds. For a more considered and elegant approach, you can fashion threshold strips from a contrasting material, say a wide strip of wood or marble tile.

Above: Luminous blue-and-white glazed tiles provide an eye-catching decorative detail inset between terra-cotta paving.

Above: Floor-level lights set in limestone follow the contour of a curved partition wall, creating nighttime drama.

The perimeter of the floor also merits attention. The flooring should be neatly laid into the angle where it meets the wall to give a clean defining line. This may entail removing the baseboards during installation. If your baseboards look battered and chipped, strip and refinish them. (Devotees of minimalism like to do without such moldings altogether, stopping the wall just short of the bottom on an inset bead, so the wall appears almost to hover over the surface of the floor. However, baseboards do protect the lower portion, so you need to consider their practical advantages.) Floor coverings should also be laid right into cupboards and closets. You may not notice the difference most of the time, but whenever the doors are opened, the lack of finish will be all too apparent.

Far left: A glossy expanse of black resin flooring makes a striking contrast to oak boards.

Above: Lights set at the base of a wall illuminate a hardwood floor and the neatly detailed transition from one area to the next.

Left: Glass flooring lends translucency and a sense of glamour to the interior. Glass must be individually specified.

An attractive floor invites floor-level living. The obvious point of reference is the traditional Japanese house, where tatami mats provide the springy, cushioned base for sitting, sleeping, and eating. In the West, we tend not to spend quite so much of our lives on the floor, but as our homes and lifestyles have become less formal and constricting, the focus has naturally shifted, literally toward the floor.

Low-level furniture, such as futons and divan beds, low coffee tables, and floor cushions encourage the use of the floor as a place for relaxing. Decorative floor-level displays also spell out the same message. Collections of beach stones, groups of indoor plants, and large urns, bowls, or platters can all provide a dramatic focal point at floor level, particularly when they are picked out by a concealed uplight or freestanding lamp. Natural sites include around and in front of a hearth or in corners out of the way of mainstream traffic.

Left: Wooden floors of all descriptions are extremely versatile, both stylistically and practically, as this maple flooring demonstrates.

Right: Original hardwood parquet is a floor worth preserving and restoring.

Below right: Water resistant and easy to maintain, tiles make ideal flooring for bathrooms and kitchens.

Bottom right: French limestone makes a cool and sophisticated floor. It is important to make sure that the subfloor can bear the weight of the stone.

Far right: Textured nonslip vinyl provides a safe covering for a metal stairway.

spills of water or grease can add to the risk of taking a tumble: carrying a hot casserole dish from the oven or stepping out of a bathtub are the types of maneuvers that demand surefootedness. And if you like to go about the house in stocking feet, the risk of slipping increases.

Changes of level increase the chances of missing your step, so special care must be taken to choose the right materials and coverings for stairs and landings. Slippery flooring is not recommended for stairs without the use of nonslip insets or nosings, and some materials, such as very coarse natural fiber coverings or shag-pile carpet, are best avoided altogether. Handrails should be provided for the elderly and any stair carpet or cover secured firmly in place to reduce the risk of tripping.

Assessing your needs

Style, character, and proportion; color, pattern, and texture — the aesthetics of choice — are crucial factors in selecting flooring. But the physical attributes of different materials and treatments must also be considered to ensure the floor performs as well as it looks.

In the following chapters, the properties of each type of flooring are covered in detail. Before you weigh the alternatives, however, it is worth reviewing some of the broad practical issues involved, then assessing your own particular requirements. Those needs will vary from household to household and from room to room.

Safety Many avoidable accidents happen in the home. Of these, falls and tumbles can be among the most serious in their consequences, especially for young children, the elderly, or the infirm. The hazards may derive from the nature of the flooring itself, from where it has been laid, or from the way it is treated and maintained.

Inherently slippery surfaces, such as terrazzo, polished linoleum, waxed wooden floors, clay or glazed ceramic tiles, present an obvious danger in certain locations. In bathrooms and kitchens,

Poor maintenance can be a cause of trouble. Loose floorboards should be nailed down and wobbly tiles securely adhered. There is no alternative but to replace frayed stair carpets to prevent heels from catching in the worn places.

Highly waxed or overpolished floors are dangerous, and it is surely worth living with a less glossy finish for the sake of safety. Unsecured rugs are also a hazard. All rugs should be laid over nonslip matting to prevent their transformation into flying carpets. This applies to the rag runner beside the bed as well as to the Oriental in the living room.

Maintenance Obviously, all floors require regular cleaning to avoid a buildup of dirt, grease, and grit; some demand additional treatment in the form of intermittent polishing, resealing, or waxing. Some types of material stain readily and irrevocably; others are more resistant. Your choice of flooring should be influenced to some extent by how much effort and expense you are prepared to invest in its care, as well as how appropriate the material is to the intended location in the home. Different materials need to be cleaned in different ways, and it is always advisable to use products and techniques recommended by the suppliers or manufacturers.

Left: The cool tones of limestone and pale oak preserve the feeling of light and spaciousness.

Below left: Mosaic tiling makes a practical entranceway.

Below: Traditional stone flooring in a classic pattern has a period flavor.

Bottom: A raised hardwood floor accentuates the airy qualities of a loft.

Right: Natural-fiber loose-laid matting adds a discreet touch to bleached hardwood.

Far right: Pebbles embedded in resin make an unusual textured surface.

Wear The degree to which a type of floor will wear is a function not only of the traffic it receives but also of how fundamentally robust it is. The concept of wear is relative. Wood, terra-cotta, and other natural materials wear well, acquiring an attractive patina of use. Subject certain synthetic flooring to the same treatment and the result may become an eyesore. Perception of wear can also be affected by the color, pattern, and texture of the material. Obviously, a pure white wool carpet is going to show every mark, whereas a flecked berber would be more forgiving.

Traffic is heaviest in circulation areas in the home — entrances, hallways, stairs, and landings — and lightest in bedrooms. In addition, there will be variations in traffic within any one space.

For example, the area beneath the dining table, where chairs are pushed back and forth, receives much heavier wear than the perimeter of the room.

Certain precautions will mitigate the effect of undue wear. Few types of flooring are immune to the intense pressure points of stiletto heels or the castors or tapering legs of heavy furniture. Protective cups will help to spread the point load of furniture legs — but the only remedy for spike heels is a change of footwear. Extra protection will also be needed in entrances and other places where grit can be tracked indoors. A wide coir mat inset across the full breadth of the hallway will catch a good deal of loose debris and absorb damp, both of which break down seals and finishes.

Stair carpets fixed by rods are more practical than fitted stair carpeting, since they can be lifted and turned to spread wear evenly. Any areas that are likely to see a high degree of wear should ideally be floored with a material that is easy to renew.

Comfort Floors that have a degree of resilience or give are less tiring on the legs and feet and therefore more comfortable than those with little resilience. Wood, cork, cushioned vinyl, linoleum, and low-pile carpet are all fairly springy underfoot, the more so if they are not laid over ungiving screeded or concrete subfloors. Hard materials, such as stone, brick, and clay tiles, have next to no resilience and are both less comfortable to stand on for long periods of time and more likely to cause breakages if anything is dropped on them.

It is worth giving some thought to texture, too. Soft or smooth materials are kinder to bare feet and young knees than scratchy, rough, or embossed surfaces.

Noise and temperature control Soft floors are the quietest way of muffling sound within a room and reducing the amount of sound that travels between floors. Hard floors amplify sound, which may cause particular problems at upper levels. A layer of sound-proofing can be incorporated under the main flooring to reduce noise further.

Continuous flooring, such as sheet linoleum or carpeting, insulates against heat loss by excluding draughts. Soft materials, such as cork and carpet, also warm up more quickly. Stone, terrazzo, clay, concrete and brick, on the other hand, are all chilly surfaces, which can be a positive advantage in a hot climate or in areas where a cooler temperature is desirable, such as in a larder, pantry, or kitchen.

Cost Price remains one of the most critical factors in the selection of flooring, but a simple cost comparison per yard can be misleading. Make sure you calculate the true finished cost of the floor you want to lay. To the price of the basic material you must add the cost of installation, plus any subfloor preparation or materials such as underlay and junction strips, the cost of sealing or finishing the floor surface, and its aftercare or maintenance (see pages 180–81). In general, be realistic: if you find you cannot afford the type of floor you really want, it is best to rethink the whole scheme rather than settle for a poorer quality version of your first choice.

Another factor to consider is the potential for refinishing. There is often little to be done about a worn synthetic covering. A worn wooden floor, on the other hand, which may well have been more expensive at the outset, can always be resanded and restored, prolonging its life and your investment. Similarly, the look of brick and terra-cotta tiled floors positively improves with age.

Most cheaper types of flooring have correspondingly shorter lives, so consider how long you need the floor to last. It is also worth thinking about how long you expect to stay in your present home; if you are renting or there is the possibility of moving in the near future, area rugs, carpets, loose-laid matting, and other types of flooring that can be taken up when you go may be the best way to spend your money.

Opting for the cheapest flooring only to find you have to replace it sooner rather than later is a false economy. Others include doing without proper professional help where it is required and skimping on preparation or underlay. There is little point in covering up a worn, pitted, or uneven floor studded with nail heads and hoping for the best. The poor quality of the underlying surface will quickly show through and cause wear and tear on whatever material you have covered it with.

Hard floors

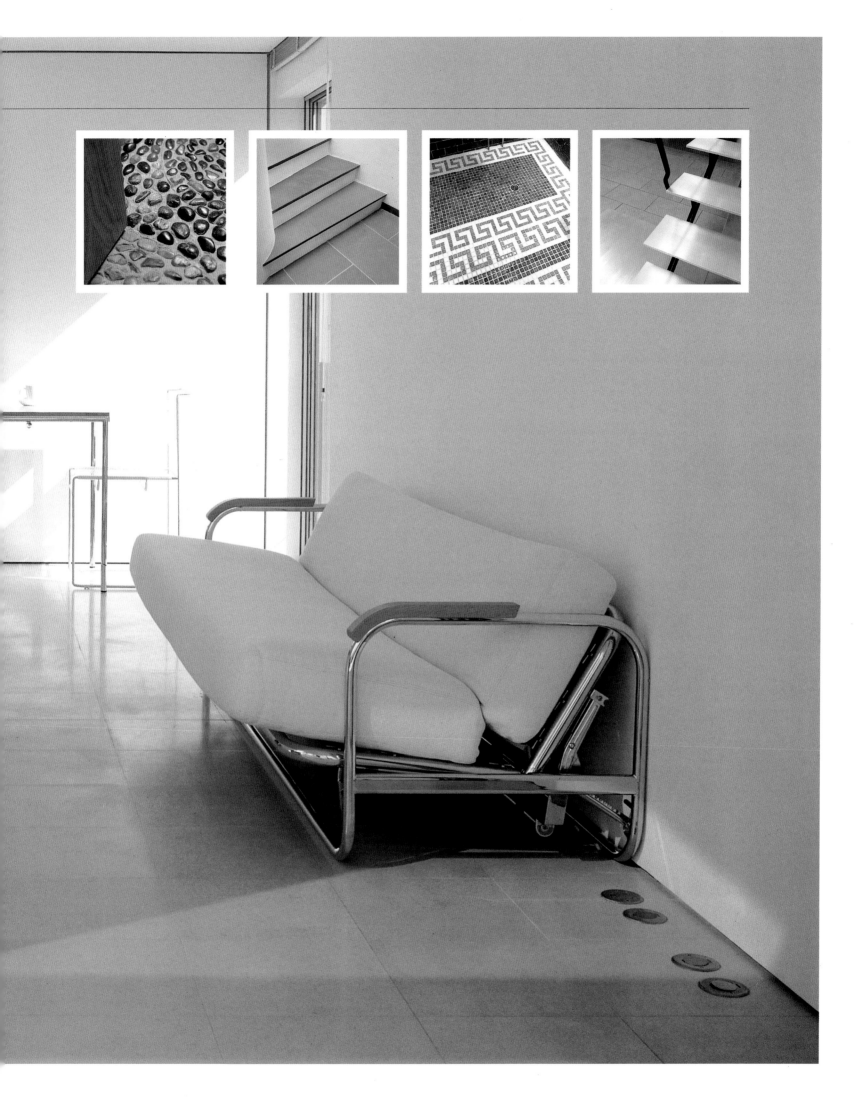

Mellow brick or opulent marble, utilitarian concrete or glittering mosaic, hard flooring materials offer an immense breadth of choice to suit any decorating scheme. Colors span the spectrum from natural neutrals to intense glazed hues; textures range from silky smooth to rippled and riven; and patterns encompass everything from speckles, flecks, and veining to representational motifs.

Yet all hard floors share certain common characteristics, many of which at first sight may seem positively disadvantageous. They are mostly chilly underfoot and can amplify sound to an uncomfortable degree. They lack resilience, which means they are tiring to stand on for long periods and anything dropped on them is likely to break. Most hard floors are heavy and require either a solid subfloor or additional reinforcement to bear the load; many demand professional laying. Some hard materials are brittle before they are laid, which increases the risk of damage in transit or installation; installation itself can be disruptive and time consuming. Most prohibitive of all, many types of hard floor have a hefty price tag.

There are, however, equally strong advantages. All hard floors convey a sense of permanence and stability. The chilliness and noisiness can be mitigated by adding a layer of rugs or matting —

Above left and right: Hard flooring encompasses a wealth of evocative materials (clockwise from top left): sophisticated terrazzo, practical hard tiles, utilitarian concrete, down-home brick, gleaming metal, pebbles, traditional marble with slate insets, glossy resin, transparent glass, and mellow terra cotta.

Right: Hard flooring can be exceptionally decorative and colorful. These painted tiles define the transition between one area and another, making a focal point of floor-level interest.

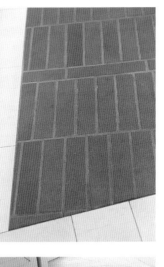

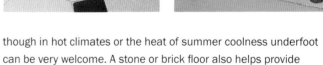

though in hot climates or the heat of summer coolness underfoot can be very welcome. A stone or brick floor also helps provide natural refrigeration in larders and storerooms.

The bulk, weight, and attendant difficulties associated with the installation of hard floors have increasingly been addressed by modern suppliers and manufacturers. Many types of stone, for example, are now available in the form of tiles, which are far easier to handle than slabs, and in thinner sections, which create less load.

Hard floors are built to last. Properly maintained, they will take a lot of punishment, which makes them ideal for areas of heavy traffic, such as hallways and passages, and areas that connect directly with the outdoors. They may cost more in terms of time, money, and effort to install, but once laid, they have the potential to last forever.

But the most persuasive argument of all remains the aesthetic one. Stone hewn from the earth has a character like no other material; fired earth is warm, rustic, and homey; ceramics alive with luminous color bring a sense of vitality to any surroundings. Even concrete or metal can be elevated from lowly utilitarian status into a work of art.

Brick

Brick is the oldest man-made building material, and as reassuring as the earth from which it derives. It is both natural and regular, standardized into comfortable units scaled to the hand, and innately domestic.

Brick began to gain in popularity as a building material in Europe as the need lessened for highly fortified castles built of stone, and instead smaller, more welcoming manor houses began to appear. In England, for example, brick was often directly substituted for stone. One early English manor, Oxburgh Hall in Norfolk, which dates from the 15th century, is entirely built of brick—walls, floors, stairs, and even a shaped brick handrail. Cheaper and easier to use than stone, brick also proved a safer material than wood. After the Great Fire of London in 1666 graphically demonstrated the inherent risks of wooden construction, brick replaced wood as the leading material for more ordinary houses and buildings.

This long history of use in the Old World gives brick a familiar quality. As a flooring material, it evokes the rustic farmhouse rather than the elegant townhouse. But new brick can be surprisingly contemporary, even sophisticated. In the work of many modern designers, the partnership of brick and wood softens and domesticates clean lines and spare interiors.

Robust, serviceable, and homey, brick is appealingly honest and unpretentious, inside or out. Indoors, brick is strictly a ground-floor treatment, since it needs a solid subfloor of significant load-bearing capacity. Visually, it works well running through a house, from hall to back door, in rooms directly connected with a backyard and in cozy country kitchens. Brick also makes a

Above left: In the right context, brick can look surprisingly stylish and sophisticated. Here the clean lines and regularity of the grid paving contributes strength to a contemporary living area.

Above center: The quirkiness of old, handmade bricks provides charm and interest. Secondhand ones can be sourced but may need to be sealed for use in heavily used conditions, especially where water may be spilt, such as kitchens and entranceways.

Above right: Brick was a common flooring material in old farmhouses and cottages. These days old brick is much in demand, for its mellow color and homey texture lend character to traditional furniture.

Right: Old brick flooring, worn smooth by the passage of generations of feet, has great appeal. It makes a practical surface for relaxed country living—ideal for rooms that lead directly into the yard.

wonderful outdoor floor for paths, steps, or terraces, and it looks good in combination with wood and stone or softened by low-growing clumps of plants.

Types and characteristics

Brick is not cheap, but it is less expensive and more readily available than many other hard materials. Flooring bricks, known as "pavers," are thinner than construction bricks—they range from ¾ inch to 2 inches thick. They are also fired at extremely high temperatures, or "overburnt," which makes them both waterproof and virtually impervious to wear. Alternatively, you can use "engineering bricks," which also have good wear resistance but are thicker than pavers. There is no law against using standard bricks as flooring, but they will eventually erode and pit into an uneven surface. Secondhand bricks have their own attractive patina of use, if you like the weathered effect. For outdoor use, make sure you choose frost-proof brick. Most characterful of all, and most expensive, are handmade bricks.

The versatility of brick testifies to its practical advantages. It is a good insulator—slow to warm, but retaining heat for a long time—a characteristic that is enhanced if brick is laid over under-floor heating. In irregularly proportioned areas, brick is also easier to use than stone slabs, for example, as it can be readily cut and shaped.

Flooring brick is exceptionally resistant to chemicals, impact, and abrasion. It is waterproof and nonslip (provided it is not sealed or polished), which makes it suitable for hallways and kitchens.

Brick comes in a wide choice of colors and surface textures. The natural warm "earthy" buffs, browns, and reds are standard, but bricks can also be blue, green, gray, and speckled, as well as ridged, ribbed, or rough textured.

Laying brick indoors is a job for the professional, demanding precision and skill. Brick requires a solid subfloor of concrete that has been cured for at least a month. It should be laid on a dampproof membrane into a deep stiff mortar bed, and the jointing needs to be done simultaneously.

Movement can be a problem with bricks (or hard tiles) bonded to a subfloor, due to changes in temperature or humidity. Joints should be wide enough to allow a small degree of shrinkage or expansion, and special movement joints may need to be incorporated at intervals throughout the floor or around its perimeter.

Patterning

The regularity and rhythm of brickwork is the source of its great appeal. There are a number of traditional patterns, which can be used indoors or out. Stretcher bond — staggered rows, as in a wall — is one of the most common patterns. It is effective over a large area, especially where there are irregular features or obstacles. Herringbone is dynamic and leads the eye on. Stack bond — where bricks are laid in straight rows — is easy to lay, orderly, and clean of line. It is best in smaller, regularly proportioned areas. Basket-weave, a pattern of alternating paired bricks, has a look of stability and enclosure. Colored bricks can be laid in evenly staggered rows to create a checkerboard effect, or more randomly, or to create a defining border.

Maintenance

Once laid, bricks need little in the way of aftercare, which is one of their great attractions as a floor material. Loose dust and dirt are simply swept up and the floor washed with mild detergent then rinsed. Flooring bricks or pavers can be polished, dressed with linseed oil or sealed — in sparing amounts. Such treatments, however, are by no means necessary and they increase the slipperiness of the floor. No dressings are recommended for absorbent bricks.

Above and below: In a hot climate brick is cool underfoot. It makes an excellent hall floor, needing little more than occasional sweeping and washing.

Right: Warm brick laid in a basketweave pattern adds rhythm and texture to sophisticated decoration.

Stone

Stone is the quintessential natural material. Its origins date back to the very formation of the Earth's crust 4,000 billion years ago, and its history of use is as old as civilization itself. Stone is embedded in antiquity. Its eternal, enduring qualities convey a sense of permanence, tradition, and stability.

Stone is one of the most varied of building materials in its applications. Its inherent strength and seeming immutability made it a natural choice for the finest or most sacred buildings. But in areas where it could be readily quarried or cut, stone also defined the vernacular architecture—mountain lodges, farmhouses, cottages, and barns that seem to grow out of their local landscape. Refined, carved, polished, and highly worked, or rugged and irregularly shaped, stone spans the full breadth of building styles.

Stone floors bring an echo of this cultural history to the interior. More importantly, very few materials can equal stone for its sheer beauty. The popular image of stone—cool, pale, and smooth—is belied by an incredible variety of colors, textures, and pattern, even within the same broad type. Limestone, for example, can range from creamy white to dappled blue, from speckly to peppered with fossils. No two slabs or tiles are alike. Even cut from the same block, each piece has its own unique surface, offering endless vitality and interest.

Like other hard materials, stone is eminently suitable for entrances and hallways, solaria, and other areas that connect directly with the exterior. Certain types also work well in kitchens and bathrooms. In living and dining areas, rectangular or square flagstones look grand and architectural, while irregular fieldstone has a rustic, country appeal. Of course, many types of stone are also excellent used as paving outdoors, for terraces, patios, paths, and in greenhouses.

Although many devotees will swear stone can be warm underfoot, it is by its very nature a cooler material than textile coverings or wood. Its coolness can be tempered by underfloor heating; once warmed, it retains heat and loses it slowly. Some types of stone are slippery, others considerably less so. All stone floors are noisy.

Above left: Contrasting stone "setts" laid in checkerboard fashion to resemble tiles in a French period bathroom decorated throughout in black and white.

Above center: Limestone comes in many colors, but the paler tones are most popular. These large slabs laid in staggered rows, generate a feeling of light and space in a modern kitchen.

Above right: Granite is one of the hardest and most expensive types of stone. Polished granite can be very slippery, but these time-worn and irregularly shaped slabs give a better textural grip.

Right: Timeless and classic, light-colored stone octagon with dark cabuchon insets are one of the most familiar of flooring patterns. The style originated in stone but is much copied in other materials.

Solid stone ranges from heavy to very heavy, depending on its thickness. Flagstones and the heavier tiles require a concrete subfloor, which tends to rule out applications at upper levels or over any suspended floor, and professional laying is recommended. Certain types, such as marble, are available in lighter, thinner, and cheaper slabs, which extends the range of applications. Some stone is porous and will stain readily unless treated with a protective coating.

Stone is available from specialist suppliers and direct from quarries; some sell only flagstones or tiles in specified sizes, other outlets will cut to order. You could also try architectural salvage yards and suppliers specializing in secondhand materials. The most expensive stone of all is antique stone, which has been reclaimed from old country houses, farms, and chateaux. With the unique patina bestowed by centuries of footsteps and scrubbing, such floors have a gentle color and texture that is impossible to re-create.

All stone is from nonrenewable sources, and some types are now very rare. It is costly to extract, work, and transport, all of which adds to the expense: the price of a stone floor (except for tiles) generally ranges from expensive to astronomical. But for those who are captivated by stone, such limitations are borne for the pleasure of living with one of the most evocative of all materials. Stone endures, and its beauty lasts for generations.

Left: Soft French limestone makes an evocative contrast to the sleek lines of a modern kitchen. Below: Hard materials, such as these flagstones, work well with the modern aesthetic.

Types and characteristics

Stone is derived from three main rock types, each one defined by its method of formation. The oldest is igneous rock, created when molten rock cooled in the earth's crust billions of years ago. It is typically dense, crystalline, and capable of taking a high polish. Granite is a good example. Sedimentary rock, such as limestone, sandstone, and travertine, is formed from deposits of sediment and organic matter and is far softer than the igneous type. The most recent, metamorphic rock, such as marble and slate, has undergone chemical change, making it extremely hard—the result of intense heat and pressure during movement of the Earth's crust.

The names of types of stone often indicate the locality where they are commonly found. For example, York stone is a sandstone from Yorkshire, England; Rocky Mountain fieldstone, Hawaiian moss rock and San Francisco cobblestone are descriptions of stones indigenous to particular regions of the United States. Other distinctions derive from the way stone is worked. Stone is generally quarried in blocks, then cut to size and format. Faces and edges may be machine sawn, often with a diamond cutter, or handworked, and finishes range from sawn and honed to highly polished. York stone and slate may be riven or split, which produces a rippled surface. In addition to squares, rectangles, and hexagons, and tiles of various dimensions and thicknesses, random natural shapes are available. Some find newly quarried stone overly reminiscent of funeral masonry, but there are predistressed varieties on the market with the soft, mellow look of old floors. Tumbling or bushmilling blurs the hard edges of the stone and produces the random surface variations associated with years of wear.

Granite is a coarse-grained rock containing feldspar, quartz, and mica, which give it an attractive crystalline appearance. It is exceptionally hard, highly resistant to wear and chemicals, and impervious to water. Granite can be near-black, blue-gray, red, pink, mottled white, and its surface is typically flecked and speckly. Its natural colors may be enhanced by flame texturing, which gives a rustic look. It is also available in a variety of other finishes, from honed to highly polished. Choose with care, though, as polished varieties may prove unacceptably slippery. Rougher textures are better for flooring; even more practical are granite setts, or paving stones, which can be laid like brick. After years of use, granite can become slippery through wear and may need to be professionally refinished. It is one of the most expensive types of stone, but tiles come at a fraction of the cost and weight. Tiles as thin as ¼ inch can be used on bathroom floors; ⅜-inch tiles in areas of light traffic.

Limestone is much softer than granite. Most types are fairly light in tone, ranging from warm neutral shades of oatmeal and cloudy white to dappled blue, green, and gray, but there are dark and near-black varieties. Surface texture is subtle yet lively. Faint veining, speckling, mottling, or flecking is typical; occasionally fossilized traces of shells or ancient marine life are apparent. Like granite, some limestone can be "flamed" to release the quartz content and the mottled patterning, which has an antique or period look.

Limestone is found all over the world. Some of the best varieties are acknowledged to be English and French in origin. Iscan and Blue English limestone are two rare, expensive blue varieties featured in many historic buildings in Europe, including St. Paul's

Granite

Limestone

Limestone

Sandstone

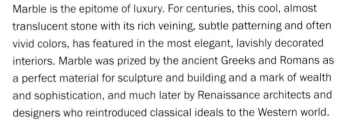

Cathedral and Westminster Abbey in London. Portland limestone, prized for its creamy whiteness, is quarried in the state of Maine; travertine, a very hard limestone, is found in the Tuscany region of Italy, and is often used for paving.

Limestone is cool and elegant. Large, even flagstones work in classic or contemporary surroundings. Some limestones wear better than others. All types are porous but may be treated to prevent staining. Limestone does not resist acid chemicals, and the harder types can become slippery with wear. It doesn't come cheap: new quarried stone will cost between two and three times as much as a good middle-price carpet.

As a floor material, sandstone is generally tougher, cheaper, and easier to maintain than limestone. Sandstone is composed largely of fine grains of quartz and comes in warm sandy shades, rich reddish browns, gray-greens, lavender, and light pearl grays. York stone is an exceptionally hard-wearing form of sandstone with a riven nonslip surface. Like limestone, sandstone is porous and stains readily but seals and polishes can make it slippery. Sandstone is available in large flagstones and in setts or plaques, and comes in various finishes—including matte, sawn, tumbled, and flame textured.

Marble is the epitome of luxury. For centuries, this cool, almost translucent stone with its rich veining, subtle patterning and often vivid colors, has featured in the most elegant, lavishly decorated interiors. Marble was prized by the ancient Greeks and Romans as a perfect material for sculpture and building and a mark of wealth and sophistication, and much later by Renaissance architects and designers who reintroduced classical ideals to the Western world.

For as long as marble has been coveted and treasured, it has been imitated. Painted faux marble floors and paneling were playful 18th-century substitutes for a rare and costly material; nowadays, marbleized floor tiles in vinyl or linoleum are the downscale equivalents. Such familiarity can breed a kind of contempt, so that even authentic marble may acquire a certain tacky or vulgar look. Marble is undoubtedly grand, but in less than grand surroundings it can look curiously cheap and showy. It may convey more of the aura of a hotel lobby or corporate headquarters than a sense of refinement. More than any other type of stone, marble demands the right context. Houses with some historical or architectural distinction are most suitable. Marble is a material for making a statement. It works well in the classic graphic contrast of black and white tiling; you need to exercise greater care if you stick to a single tone—the effect can be all too reminiscent of plastic laminate.

Far left: Small granite plaques laid in a circle on a bathroom floor.

Left center: Granite tiles can take a high polish which is uncompromisingly modern.

Near left: Cool limestone is effectively contrasted with blue-tiled walls.

Above left: A traditional limestone floor for a classic hall.

Above center: Opulent marble in a luxurious bathroom.

Above right: Black-and-white marble tiles for a handsome entrance.

Below left and right: Stone is available in a variety of colors, textures, and formats which can suit almost any location in the home – provided the subfloor will bear the weight.

Marble

Tumbled Marble

Riven Slate

Chinese Slate

Marble is a form of limestone that has crystallized under intense pressure. It is quarried in mountain ranges worldwide, but the finest examples are generally acknowledged to come from Italy. The purest marble is almost completely white. Nevertheless, it is often the imperfections, which are actually mineral deposits, that make the stone so attractive and appealing. These impurities result in a range of colors, from pink, red, green, and brown to black, and in characteristic streaking, clouding, or veining patterns. More than one color or type of pattern may be present.

Marble is generally hard wearing, although colors and patterns can become dulled by abrasion and traffic. The darker forms tend to be the hardest; creamy white alabaster, for example, the sculptor's marble, weathers badly out of doors. Slipperiness depends on the surface texture. For flooring, it is advisable to opt for a honed finish, which obviously offers a better grip than high polish.

In addition to large sheets, marble is widely available in a variety of tile formats. Usually the tile versions comprise a thin veneer of marble backed by other materials. There are also conglomerate marble tiles, composed of chippings bonded with hard polyester resin. Sheet marble is always very expensive; tiles range from fairly expensive to more affordable.

Slate, like marble, is a metamorphic rock quarried in mountain regions all over the world, from Wales to India, from Canada to China. It comes in a range of beautifully dramatic colors—dark green, blue, blue-gray, red, purple, and black—and tends to have a slick, wet look due to the high proportion of mica crystals layered through the stone. African slate is gloriously multicolored.

The presence of mica is also responsible for the fact that slate can be readily split into thin planes, a characteristic that has meant it has been widely used as a roofing material. Flooring slate is thicker than roofing sheets, but its thickness is also dependent on the way the slate is worked. Riven or split slate tends to have a slight camber, so the slabs need to be thicker and smaller than those that have been evenly sawn. Softer types of slate may have hand-worked or chipped edges, which give it a more rustic look.

Slate is by no means cheap, but it is more reasonably priced than either granite or marble, and it has other considerable practical advantages. Unlike marble or limestone, most types of slate are waterproof, which makes it excellent for outdoor paving as well as areas indoors that are likely to get wet. It is also very hard, wear resistant, and needs little in the way of aftercare. The darker shades do, however, have a tendency to show dirt and scratches.

Right: The theatrical sweep of a stairway is enhanced by the use of slabs of dark polished slate, fanning out like a deck of cards.

Slate can be finished in a variety of textures, from riven, which is nonslip, to sawn, sanded, or polished. As with other stone, the smoother finishes tend to get quite slippery when wet. In addition to regular slabs or tiles, slate is also available in randomly cut pieces that can be laid as crazy paving for a rugged, rustic look.

Pebbles and cobblestones offer a simple and charming way of paving outdoor areas. In Mediterranean countries pebble floors date back thousands of years. *Krokalia* is a Greek geometric mosaic of black and white beachstones used to create courtyard pavements of immense beauty and character. Cobbled paths, terraces, or outdoor eating areas provide a lively counterpoint to planting. The effect is found indoors, too, in entrances and even in bathrooms—very massaging for bare feet, if not highly practical.

You can buy reasonably priced cobblestones in garden centers or collect your own beach stones for free—although beachcombing could become a tedious affair for more than a small area. Stones should be smooth, evenly shaped, and similar in size. For the faint-hearted, resin-backed pebbled tiles are available that also work well as a border or as contrasting insets in a flagged floor.

Reproduction stone

Purists may throw up their hands in horror, but the difficulties and cost associated with natural stone floors have created a demand for more practical and economical simulations of the real thing. Reproduction stone has a nasty image, much of it due to the rather unconvincing stone-effect bricks sold in every garden center. Such artificial materials fool nobody; they simply lack any variation of pattern or texture from slab to slab, and the result has a depressingly mechanical appearance. However, some reproduction stone is in a different league altogether. Faithful copies, handmade from concrete, with highly realistic colors and textures and plenty of variation from "stone" to "stone," lack any hint of the ersatz. The chief advantage of reproduction stone is, of course, that it is far cheaper. Its uniform thickness also means that it is easier to lay and, sealed for indoor use, to maintain. Some flagstones are thin enough to lay over existing floors. Reproduction limestone, granite cobbles, and York stone are among the more popular simulations.

Maintenance

Porous types of stone stain readily. Expert advice from the supplier should be sought as to whether or not sealing is advisable. Sealing tends to alter the appearance of the stone. No smooth-textured stone floor should be polished—the surface will become dangerously slippery. To clean stone, scrub with warm water and a noncaustic, sulphate-free detergent, then rinse with clean water.

Above left: Slate's dark, moody tones give it a contemporary edge. Riven slate has a pleasingly rippled surface.

Above center: Slate tiles laid in a regular pattern look graphic.

Above right: A bathroom floor of beach stones set in cement recalls Mediterranean courtyards.

Right: Japanese riverbed stones set in bleached concrete and ground smooth. The effect is terrazzolike.

Hard tiles

Hand- or machine-made, glazed or unglazed, inlaid or relief textured, the diversity of hard tiles expresses a wealth of cultural traditions, from the Middle East to Mexico, from the Mediterranean to northern Europe. As practical as they are beautiful, tiles find a place in every home, and serve to complement every scheme.

The raw material of hard tiles is earth, a link preserved in the most evocative examples as warm colors and lively surface textures. Terra-cotta, that simple square of fired earth, has a history of use dating back thousands of years. Temporarily supplanted by the machine-made quarry tile in the mid-19th century, terra-cotta tiles have been rediscovered and valued for the way they age gracefully and display their craft origin and the natural quality of their basic ingredient. Ceramic tiles come in a panoply of colors, finishes, shapes, and sizes; encaustic tiles offer a wealth of decorative motifs.

The practical appeal of the tile is its durability in a format that is easy to work and handle. Like bricks, the human scale and domestic quality of hard tiles make them compatible with a range of applications. Unlike brick, the scope for decorative effects is truly vast. A tiled floor can be rustic or contemporary, provide a muted neutral background or take center stage. From the soothing rhythmic quality of plain tiles to bold contrasts of color and pattern, tiles have a liveliness that is often absent from sheet floor coverings.

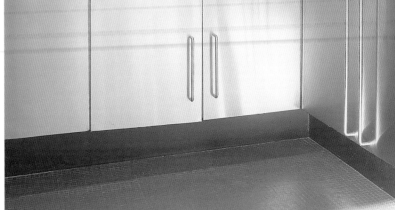

Left top: Old terra-cotta hexa-gonal tiles are full of character.

Left bottom: Terrazzo tiles feel more homey laid as a grid.

In most countries in the West, tiled floors are generally associated with hardworking areas of the home – kitchens, bathrooms, and halls. Aside from these obviously utilitarian applications, tiles can be very stylish in living rooms and dining rooms, particularly in warmer climates where their surface coolness is appreciated.

As with other flooring materials, keeping the scale sympathetic is important: larger tiles work better in generously proportioned rooms; small tiles suit more confined spaces. Floor tiling creates a sense of unity in rooms where the walls or work surfaces are also tiled, although the same tiles may not be suitable for both uses. Floor tiles are thicker and heavier than wall tiles; smooth, high-glazed tiles with a glassy surface are not safe on the floor.

Like many other natural or near-natural types of flooring, the tiled look has been widely simulated in man-made materials such as vinyl and linoleum. In the past, some tile manufacturers responded to the competition by producing lines that visually offered little more than their synthetic counterparts. There are now signs of a renewed appreciation of the intrinsic appeal of tile, which has led to a revival of historic patterns and types, a greater demand for handmade tiles, and interest in the diversity of local craft traditions.

Tiles share some of the physical characteristics of other hard flooring materials such as brick and stone. Terra-cotta apart, most varieties are cold, although this can be resolved by under-floor heating. They are all are extremely hard wearing, ceramic tiles especially, and waterproof. Maintenance is generally straightforward. On the down side, hard tiles are noisy and can become slippery when they are wet. Their lack of resilience means they are tiring to stand on for long spells and that anything dropped on them is likely to break.

The cost of floor tiles is as varied as the choice. Handmade or reclaimed antique tiles command the upper end of the price range with machine-made tiles at the other. A good-quality tiled floor costs about as much laid as the equivalent in hardwood. Laying, which often involves bedding in mortar, is work for professionals; cutting brittle tiles to fit around obstacles without damaging them is tedious work.

Far left: Glazed terra-cotta tiles in bright colors make a splash of interest in a bathroom.

Left: Hard tiles are practical and easy to clean in a kitchen.

Main picture above: Blue inset tiles sing out against a background of terra-cotta.

Right: The tiny grid of small contasting tiles is easy on the eyes.

Terra-cotta, literally "fired earth," are the oldest, and perhaps the most "natural" of all hard tiles. They have an ancient history and were widely used in Roman times. The Moors introduced tile-making techniques to Spain between the 13th and 16th centuries, and the craft spread to northern Europe and to Spanish territories in the New World. Handmade terra-cotta tiles are still produced on a small scale in many different areas of the world, using methods that have altered little over the centuries. In addition, there are antique reclaimed terra-cotta tiles on the market, some as much as two hundred years old, as well as modern machine-made versions.

From one of the most basic of all ingredients and a fairly simple manufacturing process comes a surprisingly varied, characterful product. Subtleties arise from the nature of clays and the variations in firing. Colors range from flinty gray to ocher, pink, and traditional brick red, according to region. Provençal tiles are characterized by warm pink and yellow shades; ocher is typical of Tuscany. Several colors may be present in one tile as a result of blending different clays. The type of kiln used also contributes to the final effect — wood-fired kilns tend to produce livelier tiles than gas- or coal-fired ones — and even the way the kiln is stacked can affect the quality of the finish. Mexican terra-cotta, or Saltillo, for instance, has a rough and rustic look with flame marks enhancing the warm orange color. The variety of color and texture of handmade terra-cotta is matched by slight variations in tile thickness.

Terra-cotta ages to a warm and mellow surface. Because the effect is so appealing, there is a growing market in reclaimed or antique tiles.

Terra-cotta tiles are available in a variety of shapes, among them rectangles, hexagons, and octagons, as well as the traditional 10-inch squares. Modern machine-made or extruded tiles are crisper and more contemporary looking than handmade varieties; they are sometimes supplied distressed to simulate the effect of a couple of centuries of wear. (A similar aged look can be achieved simply by laying tiles upside down.) However, the demand for authenticity is high enough for a number of suppliers, particularly in Europe, to specialize in sourcing antique terra-cotta "pammets" from old farmhouse and manor floors. On occasion these pammets can be cleaned up to display a tilemaker's mark on the reverse.

Terra-cotta tiles are supremely at home in the kitchen, where their visual warmth is matched by an ability to retain more heat than other hard flooring materials, but they also provide a distinctive base for country-style living rooms, solaria, and any area connecting with the outdoors. These unglazed tiles are porous and need sealing, which will deepen their color. The characteristic glowing patina develops with time.

Quarry tiles are made from unrefined high-silica clay that is extruded into a mold, pressed, and then burned. "Quarries," the mass-production alternative to the handmade terra-cotta tile, were first manufactured in Britain during the mid-19th century. Their popularity grew rapidly, and large quantities were exported all over the world. Originally they were unglazed, but vitrified versions are now available. For some, this eminently serviceable tile will always be Victorian, the flooring of kitchens and passageways of the English country rectory.

Quarry tiles come in the typically earthy shades of red, brown, and buff, as well as in darker colors such as blue. Very dense and hard wearing, they can nevertheless become abraded and pocked over time. Quarries are reasonably nonslip, and some varieties contain carborundum, which provides a fully nonslip surface. However, all quarries are much colder (although cheaper) than terra-cotta. Fully vitrified quarries can be used outdoors on terraces and porches. Quarries are available in a choice of sizes and thicknesses; square tiles are standard.

Above left: Quarry tiles are quintessentially Victorian, the perfect complement to the country kitchen or hallway.

Above center: Large handmade modern terra-cotta brings a natural, contemporary quality. The patina develops with time.

Above right: Old terra-cotta tiling is a floor to treasure. Color, texture, and shape of tiles vary from region to region.

Right: Cream and red terra-cotta set in a checkerboard pattern makes a sympathetic hearth in a country farmhouse.

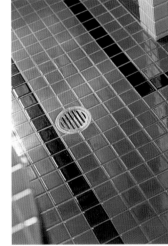

Ceramic tiles are made from refined clay, which is ground, pressed into molds under great pressure, then fired at very high temperatures. The result is an exceptionally durable tile that is very regular in dimension and coloring. This precision gives the tiles a crisp, contemporary look, accentuated by the fact that the tiling can be more closely spaced since sizes and shapes are so accurate. Understandably, ceramic tiles are most at home in clean-lined modern interiors or wherever such regularity is an asset.

Cold, hard, and wear resistant, ceramic tiles make an ungiving and somewhat tiring floor, but one that is impervious to water and most stains. Fully vitrified versions are also frost resistant. In general, ceramic tiles are slightly slippery, but nonslip versions containing silicon carbide are available, and ones with ribbed, ridged, or studded textures give a better grip. Glazed tiles are not as good at resisting wear, and matte tiles can wear down to a smoother surface. Ceramic tiles can be expensive and are generally heavy.

Ceramic tiles have regular dimensions and colors, which gives them a crisp, contemporary appearance that works well with modern interiors. Different sizes of tile create different textural effects. Very small tiles make a busy grid, which is soft-looking, like mosaic. Larger tiles are more expansive and spacious in effect. Borders or contrasting bands of color lend definition and interest.

The beauty of ceramics is the astonishing choice of colors, shapes, patterns, and textures. The familiar rustic palette of earthy shades is complemented by a whole range of more vivid colors in solid, shaded, or variegated forms, as well tones of white, black, and gray. Patterns are equally varied, from the verve and individuality of hand-painted decoration to machine-made glazed, embossed, or relief designs. Unlike terra-cotta, ceramic tiles do not acquire any discernible patina with use, but the fact that they are relatively unchanging can be welcome where a fresh, clean look is desired.

Encaustic tiles have a longer history than their link with the Victorian era suggests. Tiles inlaid with Christian, heraldic, and geometric motifs were made by monks in medieval Britain. The results are a feature of many old churches and religious buildings. The Victorian passion for the Gothic is seen in the 19th-century version of these tiles. Herbert Minton developed the mass-production process in midcentury, and by the latter decades, encaustic tiled floors had become standard for halls and porches in row houses.

"Encaustic" refers to the firing process, but it is the decoration that is so distinctive. Encaustic tiles are uniformly smooth, matte, and cool and are patterned right through. The basic material (either clay or stoneware), still in a semiliquid state, is inlaid with a pattern in another colored clay, rather than decorated or glazed superficially. Some encaustic tiles are composed of a mixture of stone and powdered marble colored with oxides; these are not fired.

Encaustic floors went out of fashion in the early 20th century, but many were simply covered over. Reclaiming an encaustic floor restores an element of architectural character to a period house. (Replacement tiles, new or secondhand, in original Victorian designs can be found, especially in Britain.) The tiles discolor slightly once laid, with clear whites softening to a duller off-white. They also stain easily before they are sealed and should be handled with care.

Patterning

The beauty of tiling is the scope it offers for creating patterns, often very simply. All tiled floors have an inherent pattern arising from the grid in which they are laid. The dynamic of this composition depends on the size and shape of the tiles and whether they are laid straight, with staggered joints, or on the diagonal.

Classic tile patterns range from octagonals or squares inset with keystones to basketweave, herringbone, and diamond. The effect of these designs can be enhanced by varying the tile type, color, or pattern: small pictorial tiles can make a charming contrast to a plain background. Some patterns, especially those that involve lozenge-shape tiles, have a Hispanic flavor; others recall medieval designs. Complex patterns with a three-dimensional optical effect, such as "tumbling block," can be created with tiles of different colors or tones. In general, the busier the pattern, the smaller the floor area should be. Complicated designs can look effective as centerpieces within a larger expanse of plainer tiling. Many suppliers offer a service to help you plan and execute special patterns.

Borders give a finished look to all tiled floors. In an irregularly shaped room, it may be better to set the border in from the wall to make an even outline rather than follow the contours of the room. Joints between border tiles should be staggered rather than aligned with the main tiling joints. Special coving or baseboard tiles make a neat seam with the base of the wall; baseboard tiles in contrasting colors or designs give the whole floor a lift.

Far left: Encaustic tiles are largely associated with the Victorian and Edwardian periods in Britain, yet their history dates back to medieval times. Gothic designs are typical, but new encaustic tiles that have organic, geometric, or pictorial themes are available.

Above left: The interlocking black-and-white pattern of this ceramic tiled floor has a retro appeal.

Above center: Classic white marble with black insets enhances the simplicity of bathroom decor.

Above right, top: A diamond inset tile: minimal yet effective contrast.

Above right, bottom: The traditional tumbling block pattern adds vitality.

Left: Patterns are easy to create in tiling simply by varying the color or size of the tile. This quarry floor uses of both types of contrast for an almost random effect.

Laying

All types of hard tile require a rigid level base or the tiles will crack. Heavier ones, such as ceramic, may place too great a load on a wooden subfloor: check with an expert if you are at all in doubt. A dampproof membrane may be needed. Tiles are either bedded in mortar or stuck with commercial adhesive, which should be water-proof if you are tiling a kitchen, bathroom, solarium, or utility area. Mix a commercial additive into the adhesive if tiles are to be laid over suspended wood floors to promote flexibility. Terra-cotta tiles should be stuck with adhesive, not bedded in mortar, to reduce "efflorescence" — the formation of salt deposits on the surface.

Lay the tiles dry first, to minimize the number that have to be cut to fit and so that grout widths can be adjusted if the tiles vary slightly. Dry laying is also vital if you are incorporating a border or a pattern. Glazed or decorative inset tiles within an area of plain tiling must be countersunk or they will abrade. Laying plastic, felt, or building paper over the subfloor, using a semidry mortar mix, and bedding in latex mortar allow a degree of movement, so tiles do not arch up. Movement joints, filled with elastic sealant, should also be incorporated, usually around the perimeter of the floor, over structural elements such as beams, and at recommended intervals.

Terrazzo

Terrazzo is an aggregate of marble or granite chips mixed with concrete or cement to form a beautiful and exceptionally hard-wearing floor. Excellent performance in areas of heavy traffic, combined with classic good looks, has won terrazzo widespread use in commercial interiors, from cafés and hotel lobbies to retail outlets. Familiarity with such applications may give terrazzo a slightly impersonal quality in a domestic setting, but it can make an elegant, even sumptuous floor for halls and other hardworking areas of the home — and in warm climates it is often favored throughout the home as a delightfully cool treatment for floors.

Terrazzo tiles and slabs are laid in much the same way as other hard tiles, with cement slurry applied to the backs before laying. Tiles are normally laid in groups separated by metal dividing strips, and they may be ground after laying.

Terrazzo is more expensive than most types of hard tile and only slightly cheaper than the best-quality stone. In practical terms, terrazzo is cold, noisy, hard, waterproof, and virtually indestructible. Hydraulically pressed tiles are extremely durable. The smooth surface is reasonably nonslip, unless it is wet, washed with soap, or polished.

Terrazzo has a much longer history than you might think. Hand-made terrazzo tiles have been produced in Mediterranean countries for over a century, where they remain a popular flooring material indoors and out. They are available in a huge choice of colors, and vary in appearance from the standard mottled mosaic of chips to crisp geometric designs that lend themselves particularly well to modern settings, a pleasing complement to chrome fixtures, pale wood, and glass.

There are several formats. Terrazzo can be mixed and laid in situ, or laid as tiles or slabs. In all cases, laying is professional work. In situ, terrazzo is troweled onto a solid concrete base or onto screed bonded to a concrete base to form panels within brass or zinc dividing strips. It is then ground to produce a smooth finish, washed, filled with cement paste, cured, and polished.

Maintenance

General maintenance is straightforward. Terrazzo is best washed with warm water and a little scouring powder; soap makes the surface too slippery. Water-based sealants will protect against staining. Avoid polish containing wax.

Above left: Terrazzo is sleek and contemporary. The link with public spaces has given its crossover into the home environment an additional exciting edge.

Above center: Terrazzo owes its luxurious appearance to ingredients such as marble chippings, colored glass, and stones ground smooth.

Above right: Patterns and motifs can be achieved using contrasting colors. Laid in position, terrazzo can be expensive.

Right: The smaller scale of these terrazzo tiles suits the domestic setting. The material is simple to maintain and very robust, making it ideal for such hardworking areas as entrances and kitchens.

Mosaic

Mosaic is true floor-level art. Small cubes bedded in mortar in decorative or geometric designs give mosaic an irresistible intricacy and delicacy. The scale of individual pieces and the variations of light catching on their surfaces create a gentle, almost blurred effect. Mosaic floors are hard, but their appearance is soft.

Any size floor can be covered with mosaic, although in practice it tends to be used on a smallscale—in bathrooms, in hallways or as decorative panels inset within a larger tiled or flagged floor. The technique is exceptionally labor intensive, which also accounts for the expense of a commissioned mosaic floor. Simple geometric mosaics are not impossible for the amateur to tackle, but for more complex patterns, you need a mosaic artist to design and carry out the work. A good artist will be able to show you examples of other projects and produce an original design to suit a particular location.

Mosaic flooring is generally composed of cubes, or *tesserae,* of marble, stone, terra-cotta, or unglazed colored ceramic. Different materials can be combined within the same mosaic. Vitreous glass mosaic is not suitable for flooring because it fractures easily under point loads and can be too slippery. Honed marble is generally used in preference to highly polished varieties. Marble and other stone *tesserae* tend to vary in thickness, making them harder to install than ceramic mosaic, which is evenly dimensioned.

Mosaic shares many of the characteristics of other hard floors: it is durable, noisy, and fairly cold. However, the natural key supplied by the myriad grouting joints means that mosaic is far less slippery than floors made of larger tiles or slabs of the same material.

Below: Mosaic pavements featured in buildings throughout the Roman Empire. Current designs are often inspired by antique examples.

Center: A Greek key pattern adds a classical flavor to this mosaic.

Center right: A mosaic surface shimmers as light catches on the tiny cubes of stone and tile.

Far right: Geometric patterning is easier for amateurs to create than full-scale pictorial designs.

The grouting also contributes far more positively to the overall effect. Intensely colored mosaic is enhanced by dark grouting; light grouting has a tendency to dull strong colors and to make designs look more fragmented. Light grouting makes pale mosaic look more seamless; dark grouting gives a more drawn or graphic effect.

Laying

Mosaic can be heavy. It is best laid on a concrete subfloor, but it can be laid on a suspended wood floor covered with a layer of marine plywood to provide a stable, inflexible base. A deep bedding of mortar will take up any discrepancy in thickness. Ceramic mosaic can be stuck in a thin bed of adhesive over a flat screed. Check with an expert if there is any doubt about load-bearing capacity.

There are two main ways to create a mosaic floor. One is the direct method, which involves sticking in the individual pieces one by one. It is best used only for small areas, as it is time consuming, and restricted to simple designs, so that there is less room for error. The most practical is the reverse method. The mosaic is first stuck to paper with water-soluble glue, with the finished surface face down. The back of the mosaic is then grouted or covered with a sand and cement slurry to fill in the gaps and the mosaic pressed, right side up, on the floor. The paper is wetted to dissolve the glue and peeled away, and the mosaic is washed to remove all traces of glue and left to "go off," or cure, before final grouting.

The great advantage of the reverse method is that it minimizes installation time, since the lengthy process of cutting and piecing the design can take place away from the site before the mosaic is slotted together in finished sections. As the complete floor is built up from sections, care must also be taken to fit these together properly so that joins are not visible.

Maintenance

Mosaic, particularly marble mosaic, must not be highly polished after it is laid or the natural key provided by the difference in texture between the mosaic and grouting will be lost and the surface will become dangerously slippery. Wash with a gentle detergent.

Above left: A concrete floor at its most basic: defiantly brutal.

Above center: Concrete studded with pebbles has a quirky look.

Above right: Concrete can be variously treated to alter its color and texture – here it is painted to simulate old flagstones.

Left: For such a hard material, concrete can be visually soft.

Right: Polished concrete, edged in black, makes a stark modern floor.

Far right: Concrete's appeal as a modern floor is its uncompromising and strong sculptural quality.

Concrete

Concrete is the ultimate workhorse floor, utilitarian, basic, even a little brutal. Its popular image as a soulless, harsh material is not undeserved in its raw state, but screeded and painted, waxed, textured, or coated, it can be transformed into a sleek, sophisticated finish of considerable stylistic merit.

Concrete is a blend of cement, aggregate, and sand. It is available in slabs or tiles, or mixed and laid directly on site. Its main domestic use is as a subfloor for other, generally heavy, coverings, or as practical but unlovely flooring in utility areas, cellars, and garages. There are, however, a variety of ways in which concrete can be lifted out of the ordinary. Some require the rough concrete base to be covered with a smoother sand and cement screed. For a finish not unlike terrazzo, special aggregate can be incorporated in

the mix and the laid floor then ground and polished after it has set. An unusual effect can be achieved by scoring patterns or embedding pebbles while the concrete is still wet, then sealing and waxing.

Concrete must be sealed to prevent the surface from dusting. Special concrete floor paints, available in a variety of colors, give an attractive and durable finish. Concrete can also be colored with the same pigments used for plaster for a soft, matte look. Several coats of acrylic or epoxy resin result in a hard reflective finish that is very tough and chemical resistant. Other types of resin or aggregate toppings are textured and nonslip. Most of these finishes are designed principally for industrial or commercial applications and, like the floor itself, should be laid by a professional for the best results. Once laid, though, concrete needs little more maintenance than scrubbing with hot water and detergent.

Painted a glossy neutral tone, concrete achieves a high level of sophistication. The reflective sheen adds spaciousness and light.

Concrete's tough aesthetic works well with the clean lines and metal finishes of an industrial-style kitchen.

Metal

Another migrant from commercial or industrial settings, metal flooring brings a sleek contemporary edge to the interior. The hard shiny surface, with its aeronautical associations, makes a bold statement in a modern space. It is available in sheet and tile form and is normally textured with raised patterns to provide a nonslip surface. Aluminum and galvanized steel are the most commonly used metals; zinc is too soft. Aluminum is up to three times lighter than galvanized steel and does not rust.

Metal sheet can be laid over a level wood or concrete subfloor and may be either bonded with adhesive or screwed and plugged in place. If the floor is to be mechanically secured, a little adhesive should also be applied to take the flexion out of the floor and

prevent it from rattling when you walk across it. Even so, the surface will be noisy and cold underfoot. Metal flooring can be sealed and is best maintained by washing with water and detergent.

Glass

Glass flooring is the ultimate in drama. At upper levels, as a mezzanine walkway, glass has a "look-no-hands" quality that adds an exciting dimension to the interior and allows clear views through a normally vertically divided space. Its application in domestic contexts is not widespread, though – and it is expensive.

The type of glass suitable for flooring is thick annealed float glass, rather than toughened glass. Every glass floor should be individually specified to meet loading requirements, but in most household situations adequate strength is provided by a ¾-inch-thick top layer laminated to a ⅜-inch base layer. To keep weight and

Above: Metal and glass heighten the drama of stairways.

Center: Metal laid in tile form makes an unusual floor for a dining area.

Top right: The ultimate in glass flooring: display cases topped with glass laminate.

Bottom right: Glass needs friction bars to be a safe walkway.

maneuverability within reasonable limits, it is usual to work in yard-square panels. Glass walkways must be supported on all four edges by a wooden or metal frame that entirely encloses the thickness of the glass. Glass cannot be butted up against another hard material; edge cushioning in the form of neoprene rubber must be included and the rubber must be hard enough to withstand compression. To counter the extreme slipperiness of the floor, it is usually necessary to have friction bars sandblasted at intervals across the surface.

Wooden flo

Waxed oak parquet, dark stained maple boards, pale ash strips, or honey-colored pine, wood is one of the most beautiful and accommodating of all flooring materials. It is also a material with which we have an instinctive rapport, born out of centuries of familiarity. Wood has found a role in almost every aspect of the construction, detailing, decoration, and furnishing of houses, from doors to window frames, from baseboards to balustrades, from chests of drawers and kitchen tables to—floors.

Few materials are so versatile or so commonplace. But this familiarity has neither bred contempt nor indifference; wood has proved remarkably immune to the swings of interior design or architectural fashion, and is equally at home in the penthouse suite and the rural farmhouse.

The eternal appeal of wood owes much to the fact that it derives from a natural, living source. The pattern of growth evident in knots and grain gives wood an essential vitality and variety, which makes it easy to live with in large doses. No two boards are alike, no two species are alike. Wood, in fact, is a family of materials with related but different characteristics. Like all natural materials, wood ages well and, with sympathetic care, it lasts well, acquiring a depth of character that money cannot buy nor manufacturers simulate.

The variety of tone or color, texture, and density of bare wood is complemented by a choice of formats, from sheets, strips, and boards to mosaic tiles, blocks, or parquet. The rhythm and scale of each format have an impact on the overall appearance of the floor.

Above: Plain, "unfinished" floorboards provide a good counterpoint to furnishings with a period flavor. The light tone of old oak increases the sense of light and spaciousness.

Above left: Pine floorboards have been "ebonized" to create a graphic, glossy surface in a minimalist's apartment.

Left: Hardwood flooring is a classic contemporary surface. Beech is currently one of the more popular woods.

Small-scale tiles and blocks have a busier, more enclosing look. Wide boards look rugged and rustic, narrow strip flooring has a seamless quality. Then there is the decorative dimension. Wood can be simply sealed and left to speak for itself or treated as a blank canvas and bleached, stained, painted, and stenciled. In addition, it provides an attractive setting for rugs and mats.

Neither hard nor soft, but somewhere in between, a wood floor offers many practical advantages, the best, in some ways, of both worlds. It is cooler and "breezier" than carpet, but warmer than stone and hard tiles. Unless laid over concrete, most wooden floors have plenty of give, which makes them comfortable to walk and stand on and less liable to cause breakages when something is dropped on them.

Above center: Floorboards have been lightened with white paint enhance the sense of purity and simplicity in a generously scaled bathroom.

Far right: The rich hues of an elm floor can look just as well in an uncompromisingly contemporary context as in a more traditional setting.

Left: New French oak floorboards add just enough warmth to what could otherwise be an austere color scheme.

Wood is not brutally noisy, but it is no guarantee of a quiet life. A suspended plank floor in a room with few soft furnishing accessories can add to the echoing quality, while expanses of bare boards at upper levels can be quite noisy in the rooms below. If you live in an apartment, consider your downstairs neighbors before opting for a bare wood floor, otherwise good relations could become strained. It is, though, easy to muffle the sound with a layer of rugs or matting on those areas of the floor that take most of the daily traffic and still enjoy the beauty of exposed wood around the perimeter; in extreme circumstances, underfloor soundproofing can radically decrease noise levels. But for many people, the odd creaking board or squeak of parquet is all part of the evocative appeal of wood.

Wood comes in most price ranges. New lumber, especially new hardwood, is expensive, but it will easily outlive, say, a top-of-the-line carpet. A solid oak floor should last for generations. In the middle range, wood strip and block flooring are available from major outlets, while cheapest of all are manufactured sheets such as plywood, which can look surprisingly stylish. Veneered flooring is cheaper than the equivalent solid wood version, but correspondingly it has a much more limited life, since the veneer is usually too thin to be stripped and refinished once it has worn. Renovated boards generally demand more hard work than hard cash.

Above far left: Inlay of cherry fruitwood makes a sumptuous finishing touch.

Above: Herringbone parquet makes a lively contrast to the gridded pattern of the paneled walls.

Above left: Edging pine with a darker inset adds a neat detail.

Left: Gleaming oak boards match the modern feel of metal fittings.

Wood is more demanding than a hard floor in terms of care and maintenance. It is by no means proof against all damage, even when properly sealed. Grit tracked in on the soles of shoes wears down the seal and allows in moisture and dirt; spike heels and narrow furniture legs are incredibly destructive. Even under normal circumstances, sealants and finishes need to be renewed from time to time. Really bad patches of wear may mean that the entire floor will need to be refinished. But the result is a long life of good looks.

There are few areas of the home where a wood floor would not be welcome, either stylistically or practically. Both functional and beautiful, wood works as well in kitchens as in living rooms, dining rooms, bedrooms, and playrooms. Its susceptibility to changes in humidity, however, means its use is not recommended where exposure to water and steam — in poorly ventilated bathrooms, for example — would inevitably compromise its durability. All-weather decking can extend wooden flooring right out onto the veranda, terrace, and beyond.

Left: 18th-century refinement in wood. Superb oak marquetry inlaid with Brazilian rosewood creates floor-level artistry.

Right: In some contexts, plain particleboard can be elevated to the status of a final floor.

Below: The width of this planking is characteristic of early construction.

Below right: A classic with a modern edge. Woodblock of light fruitwood with black insets.

Wood is a good unifier. In dual-purpose rooms or open-plan spaces, a wooden floor provides a cohesive background without the sometimes deadening sameness of wall-to-wall carpeting or sheet flooring. The rhythm provided by the individual units—the boards, tiles, parquet blocks, or strips—means that even large expanses of wood retain a homey quality.

After centuries of use, we show no signs of tiring of this classic material. In fact, as interest grows in natural sources and products, wood has acquired a heightened level of appreciation and has

become a more popular choice than ever for flooring. With this shift in emphasis has come an equivalent concern to make sure that the lumber used in the home should be from sustainably managed plantations and other renewable sources that do not lay waste to irreplaceable rain forests or indigenous woodlands.

New wood

Classic and contemporary, new wood is one of the most elegant of flooring materials. Physically warm, aesthetically cool—sheer quality underfoot. But stylishness does not rule out more down-home virtues. The best wood floors mellow to a comfortable patina that is as pleasing as the finish on a cherished piece of furniture.

"New wood" encompasses a wide range of species and formats, with equivalent variations in price, durability, suitability, and appearance. Solid hardwood floors are expensive and require professional laying and informed selection as to species, but they are extravagantly beautiful and exceptionally durable. At the other end of the spectrum are ready-made wood floors, which come with a mass-market price tag and can be laid by an amateur. But, as always, you get what you pay for, and the downside to these more affordable alternatives is a relatively short life that often cannot be prolonged by refinishing. Nevertheless, with proper care, even the cheapest wood offers the pleasure of contact with a natural material and the appealing blend of associations that wood inspires.

The densest woods are the most resistant and hard wearing. Some wood is strong and hard enough to function as industrial flooring, able to withstand the heavy loads of factory machinery or the incessant traffic of a school hallway. Needless to say, such performance levels are never required in the home, but different types of wood do vary in their practical characteristics, and some are better in certain contexts than others.

Durability is also a function of how the lumber is worked. The toughest is end grain, followed by quarter sawn, where the wood is cut radially for more even grain pattern and greater stability. Plain sawn lumber doesn't wear as well and may be less attractive (plain-sawn softwood, for example, is very knotty), but it is cheaper and more readily available. Veneered boards or tiles are least durable of all.

Top left: Different colored woods laid in broad bands make a subtle contrast of tones.

Top right: Hardwood on a solid stairway adds texture and warmth.

Above and center: Strips and blocks provide rhythm and interest

Opposite: Hardwood laid herringbone fashion accentuates the transition from area to area.

Left: Wood flooring is a good unifier in open-plan spaces, softening clean modern lines with its warm, natural tones.

Right: The pale tones of oak flooring make a perfect surface in a modern house by the sea, with its dramatic light-filled vistas.

Below: New hardwood flooring, such as this oak strip, has the potential to improve with age, amply repaying the initial high investment.

Left: The even tones of beech make it a popular, easy-to-live-with choice for modern interiors. It is strong and very hard wearing. Press-dried beech can be harder than oak, and it is less expensive.

Types and characteristics

Lumber species broadly fall into two categories: softwoods and hardwoods. Softwoods, as their name implies, are generally less durable than hardwoods. They are also widely available and cheap. The two main softwoods are pine and fir. Their principal uses are as replacement wood for original softwood floors that have become damaged beyond salvation and in new construction. Hardwoods, which are slow to grow, are always more expensive than softwoods and display an incredible variety of color, pattern, and texture. New wood floors are generally made of hardwood, which may be either in solid or veneer form.

In recent decades, many hardwood species, particularly from tropical regions, have become endangered. Uncontrolled deforestation has destroyed vast areas of rain forest around the world, with disastrous ecological consequences. Some of the species most at risk include afromosia, iroko, keruing, mahogany, sapele, utile, and teak, all of which have flooring applications.

It is up to you, the consumer, to be responsible when choosing wood. In general, it is advisable to avoid buying any imported tropical wood unless it has been produced on a managed plantation and is certified as such by the Forest Stewardship Council. This international body keeps track of properly managed forestry projects around the world which provide sustainable sources of times as well as livelihoods for local communities.

New woods suitable for flooring from temperate forests in Europe and North America include:

Ash Pale, tough with a coarse texture and straight grain. Good for general use.
Beech Attractive, light toned, and very strong and durable. Widely used in block flooring. If press-dried it can be harder than oak.
Birch Pale, finely textured. Not strong. Commonly used as plywood.
Cherry Fine grained, rich warm color with slight pinkish tinge.
Chestnut Exceptionally strong and durable.
Elm High water resistance and dark rich color. Very strong.

Lime Pale, straight grained, and fine textured. Good for general use.
Maple An excellent flooring wood. Will withstand heavy traffic; is often used as flooring in museums, schools, and ballrooms. Reddish tinge.
Oak (American, English, and French varieties) The classic flooring wood. Coarse grained. Strong and durable. Resists water, rot, and pests.
Pine Light softwood, available in various grades. Honey toned when sealed. Less durable than hardwood but very economical. Must be treated against rot and woodworm before use.
Sycamore Light toned but takes staining well. General use.
Walnut Matures to rich color. Wavy grain.

Of these, ash, beech, maple, and oak are the most common hardwoods used in flooring production. Many flooring manufacturers produce boards in a variety of finishes and colors, so the same species may be offered in its natural tone, bleached, oiled, lacquered, colored, or stained to resemble a tropical wood. Some strip flooring is treated with acrylic hardener to increase its durability. In addition, boards may be supplied untreated so that you can apply your own environment-friendly finishes.

All wood must be correctly seasoned before use. Seasoning is the process by which newly cut wood gradually loses moisture until it reaches an equilibrium with the atmosphere, shrinking as it does so. If you laid green boards in a centrally heated room, before long the wood would have shrunk considerably, possibly warping and splitting in the process. Similarly, wood that has dried out too much will absorb moisture in a humid location and swell. Flooring lumber is generally kiln-dried to a moisture content of 10% or less. Major flooring manufacturers will supply wood that is ready to use; in other cases, you may need to keep the wood in the room in which it will be laid for a period of ten days to two months in order for it to acclimatize fully. The amount and type of heating you have in your home can be critical. If you like the room thermostat turned up or, particularly if you have underfloor heating, the wood will need to have a lower moisture content.

Golden birch American Oak Maple American Elm Ash Cherry birch Beech

Top: The spare, uncluttered lines of a contemporary kitchen are accentuated by light beech flooring.

Above left: Pirainah pine laid herringbone fashion and edged with a darker strip inlay makes a classic entrance.

Above: New wood softens the otherwise stark features of this small room. Narrow strips work best in a restricted space.

Above right: Humble pine gains distinction laid in wide boards, then sanded and sealed for a hard finish.

The terminology for wood flooring can be confusing. "Parquet" is sometimes used synonymously with strip flooring; "block" and "parquet" are also used interchangeably. "Boards" generally refer to softwood floorboards; "woodstrip" can mean anything from a length of hardwood of similar dimensions and thickness to thin overlay.

Parquet or block flooring has a long history of use, reaching the height of artistry in the 17th- and 18th-century chateaux of France. Many chateaux boasted their own individual designs, created in position and resembling the finest inlaid furniture. Composed of small strips or blocks of hardwood, most typically oak, parquet is laid in patterns that range from the familiar herringbone to more intricate designs featuring interlocking lozenge shapes or woven basketweave.

Modern parquet is supplied tongued and grooved or doweled and is made from a variety of different hardwoods. Solid wood parquet can be refinished, providing the tongues or dowels are not too near the surface.

Other forms of parquet or block consist of solid elements glued together or a hardwood veneer over a softwood base. Some of these products can be loose laid; others laid on a dry existing floor, provided it is perfectly flat. For an *ancien régime* look, there are suppliers specializing in reclaimed parquet.

Wood mosaic Essentially these are wooden floor tiles which consist of thin strips of wood glued together to form squares and bonded to a base of scrim, felt, or adhesive backing. Some are faced with paper or a membrane that is removed after laying. A tile or mosaic panel usually consists of four squares set at right angles to each other to form a basketweave pattern. The size, thickness, and type of wood vary.

Panels are usually tongued and grooved and may be adhesive-backed or stuck in place. Mosaic has good resistance and is less susceptible to movement due to changes in moisture levels. It does have a rather dated appearance, however, and lacks the grandeur of solid wood flooring or the elegance of parquet.

Woodstrip Hardwood strip varies in thickness, length, and width. Generally the larger the dimensions, the more expensive the wood. Narrow woodstrip flooring can look a little institutional, uncomfortably reminiscent of a school gymnasium; wide, long boards are more luxurious. Many manufactured floors consist of strips glued together to resemble boards.

Thick planks or strip floors can be laid over joists like floorboards; thinner strip flooring must be laid over a solid subfloor or a dry, flat existing floor. Both types are usually supplied tongued and grooved

Opposite page: Woodblock flooring made of end grain, the hardest and most durable cut, makes a practical surface in a dining area.

Above top: Pale wood has an appealing timeless quality.

Above: Beech woodblock unifies connecting and living spaces.

Left: The rhythm of wood mosaic is complemented by natural-fiber rugs. A layer over the areas most walked upon lessens the noise of bare wood.

so they fit together without leaving any gaps. One international supplier offers thick strip flooring that can be laid like ship's decking; the boards are tapped together, with colored neoprene in the seams compensating for any movement and reducing slipperiness.

Thickness is a critical factor and ranges from about ⅜ inch to 1 inch. Woodstrip of medium thickness can be refinished if it is solid wood and the tongue is well below the surface, but woodstrip that consists of a layer of thin hardwood veneer over a softwood or composition wood base cannot be sanded.

Manufactured strip flooring or overlay is designed to be easy to install and maintain, as well as economical: at the cost, however, of a certain degree of authenticity. Some laminated strip flooring has only the merest skin of wood facing; the effect, inevitably, is rather synthetic. High-pressure laminates can withstand heavy-duty traffic, spike heels, and cigarette burns.

Veneered wood floors backed with cork for extra resilience and comfort are also available. Strips as thin as ⅛ inch can be glued to subfloors or, twice as thick, loose laid as a floating floor over an existing one. Like laminates, they are very resistant to damage by heavy furniture or high heels and require no subsequent varnishing. The cork cushioning makes them ideal for laying over concrete, and they are also quiet, no-slip, antistatic, and hypoallergenic. Purists might quibble that such floors retain a manufactured quality that lacks the depth of character of solid wood.

Left: Woodchip is not generally recommended for flooring purposes, but it makes a lively temporary covering.

Far right: Plywood panels have been screwed in place over old floorboards and are completely in keeping with this modern setting.

Laying

Laying a new wood floor is usually professional work. Good hardwood represents a significant investment that could all too easily be spoiled by a botched amateur job; intricate parquet patterns demand skill. The exception is manufactured strip flooring, which is fairly straightforward to install (see pages 174–75).

Subfloor requirements vary. Boards and thick woodstrip can be laid on joists or battens, which means that pipes and cables can be run under the floor. Maximum spans are dictated by the thickness of the wood. Boards and thick woodstrip can also be used over underfloor heating. Thinner woodstrip, mosaic, and some types of parquet can be laid over any dry, flat floor. Existing floorboards should be covered with plywood or cardboard. Concrete may need to be covered with a dampproof skin or resilient underlay. Solid parquet is usually laid on concrete.

Left: Birch plywood, laid in large sheets, creates a stylish floor. Plywood may not be as long-lived as hardwood, but it is so economical that reflooring is perfectly affordable.

Although plywood is man-made, it is wholly wood—not synthetic in any sense. It is composed of thin sheets of wood glued together under pressure, and its strength derives from the fact that sheets are layered at right angles to each other. Composition varies, with birch being the most common ingredient. Birch, which is not a particularly strong wood, gains strength in this format. Types of plywood suitable for flooring include those that are birch-faced or maple-faced on a softwood base and those that are solid birch.

Plywood panels are widely available; the best sources are lumberyards. Thicknesses of up to ¾ inch can be supplied cut into squares and tongued and grooved for easy laying . Provided the size of panels is not too unwieldy, laying a plywood floor can be successfully tackled by a competent amateur. Plywood is sufficiently flexible to accommodate slight unevenness in existing subfloors. It can be laid on boards or joists if it is thick enough or bedded in bitumen on concrete. Make sure the grain faces in the same direction. Sand lightly and seal thoroughly with a good lacquer to bring out the warmth and luster of the material. Alternatively, plywood can be stained or painted before sealing.

Plywood is not long lasting. The cheapest, veneered or faced, types will wear quickly; those that are birch throughout have a slightly longer life and can be gently sanded.

Plywood

Plywood has long been a byword for the flimsy and makeshift, a manufactured wood fit only for temporary or utilitarian uses. But in recent years the material has been rediscovered: cheap and nasty has undergone a transformation into cheap and cheerful chic. What was once considered appropriate only as a base for subfloors has emerged as a stylish covering in its own right.

Early modernists, such as Le Corbusier and Mies van der Rohe, were among the first to appreciate the suave potential of this machine-made wood; prewar, plywood was used for flooring, among many other applications. During the 1950s and '60s, the material was more or less eclipsed by other manufactured wooden flooring products, as well as wood-effect simulations in vinyl.

The latest reincarnation of plywood has come about as the result of a renewed appreciation of its practical and aesthetic qualities. Plywood is modern, natural, and agreeably utilitarian, as opposed to strip flooring, which can sometimes take on more glitzy, even commercial overtones.

Above: Old wood lends character to contemporary furnishings arranged in a converted warehouse space.

Above left: The simplicity of original wooden flooring makes a perfect complement to period decor.

Left: The textural character of these walnut boards arises from the fact that they were hewn with an adz, rather than machine sawn.

Below left: Bare untreated boards make a rough-and-ready floor.

Opposite page: To create this "period" floor, old oak boards were laid at varying heights and spacing, then scratched and bleached for a distressed surface, rather than sanded smooth.

Old wood

In the same way wall-to-wall carpeting defined the new comfort and informality of the Western lifestyle in the 1950s and '60s—along with the built-in kitchen and open-plan arrangement—stripped floorboards have become a contemporary decorating standard, and for very good reasons. Renovated floorboards are cheap and characterful, versatile and practical, and effectively make a very easy match with any style in the home decorator's repertoire. Old wood offers a naturally sympathetic complement to period looks, but its spare, structural quality works equally well in ultramodern interiors.

When the vogue for stripped floors began, renovating old wood went hand in hand with restoring period features and preserving architectural character: an antidote to the many unthinking and unsympathetic conversions of the postwar period. More recently, such treatment has more or less shed its worthy or historic overtones as homeowners have recognized that a restored wood floor is simply the easiest, and one of the most affordable, means of achieving a pleasant, natural surface that can withstand a fair amount of wear and tear.

The period credentials of bare floorboards do not always stand up to close inspection. Eighteenth-century interiors often displayed simple planked flooring but without the modern array of sealants and varnishes, the color and overall effect would have been a little different. In the Victorian era, when many of today's stripped, bleached, or waxed boards were first laid, most wooden flooring in the main rooms would have been fairly well covered by rugs and area carpeting; any exposed wood was generally painted a dark color to blend in with the background. Stripped floorboards, however authentic they may seem, reveal more accurately a modern desire for simplicity and a renewed interest in natural materials; one day they may seem as indelibly late 20th century as the antimacassar is High Victorian.

Renovating old wood, by and large, is not expensive—a powerful recommendation for many new homeowners with a sense of style and limited budgets. Stripping old boards that have been hidden from view under a layer of old carpet or linoleum must rank as one of the most common decorating projects for those in proud possession of an older property. But do not underestimate the amount of effort involved. Sanding, stripping, and finishing original wooden floors demands a certain degree of expertise and plenty of muscle. If in doubt, it is always best to bring in the professionals to do the work for you.

The type of original wood flooring most commonly encountered in houses built in the 19th and early 20th centuries are pine boards laid horizontally across rooms so that they run at right angles to the wood joists. Pine, which is a softwood, has long been a standard constructional material. Softwoods, by their very nature, sand more

Above: Stripped Columbian pine creates a warm and uncluttered base in a contemporary living area, and is a good partner for the irreverent leopard-print carpeting on the stairway.

readily than hardwoods. In older, especially rural, properties, floors may be made of a hardwood, such as oak, often in wide planks. Original parquet flooring is also likely to be made of solid hardwood and can be sanded and refinished in the same way as boards.

Restoring old wood
Once the floor has been given a good overhaul—repaired, prepared, sanded, and stripped of previous finishes—there are numerous options available for the final finish, ranging from those that preserve the grainy appearance and tone of the wood to painted effects of various kinds that cover up the wood's character but widen the scope for color and pattern.

Above: Original herringbone parquet makes a stylish floor in a dining area. Old parquet is solid wood and can be reclaimed and restored in much the same way as floorboards.

Above center: Stripped pine works equally well with traditional decorating schemes.

Above right: Original oak floorboards provide depth of character.

Below left: Kitchens see a good amount of traffic, but wooden floors can withstand a fair degree of wear. These stripped boards are a counterpoint to the gleaming metal fixtures.

Below right: Reclaimed pine block flooring makes a heavy-duty surface for a modern island kitchen. Blocks have more utility character than either boards or woodstrip.

Whether an old wood floor has been hidden under other coverings or subject to years of traffic and wear, your first task is to assess its condition and carry out all necessary repairs. This could mean treating rot or structural failure, or simply securing loose boards or filling gaps (see Remedial Work, pages 164–65). Nails that have worked their way to the surface need to be sunk, and the wood cleaned of any old wax, polish, or paint. Paint splashes can be removed with chemical stripper and a scraper or sandpaper. If the floor is already painted, you will also have to strip off as much paint as possible before sanding to avoid clogging up the sandpaper. Chemical strippers are quite expensive, and need to be handled with care, but they are undoubtedly the best solution for tackling large or tricky areas.

At this stage you will be able to assess whether or not the floor requires machine sanding. In rare cases, where the wood is even and has been well protected or if you intend to paint it anyway, hand sanding may be all that is needed, working in the direction of the

Top: Parquet flooring has an air of solidity and permanence. Parquet features in many older apartment blocks, and provides an evocative, traditional surface that is worth preserving.

Above: Woodblock flooring of mixed woods, with cherrywood inlay used to create an intricate border, lends architectural distinction that marries well with the rich decorating colors.

Left: Gleaming cherry and pear-wood block flooring provides retro appeal and interest that comple-ment the early modernist furnishings in this work area, and prevents the room from appearing too stark or clinical.

Above: Old parquet has a welcome patina and character. Specialist outlets can supply original solid parquet salvaged from old houses and aparments. Slight unevenness of surface and spacing is all part of the charm.

grain. Herringbone parquet must be sanded in both directions, following the pattern. In most cases, renovating old wooden floors will require machine sanding to deep clean, to remove all vestiges of previous finishes, and to provide a level surface. Sanding removes the top layer of wood, and the poorer the condition of the floor, either in terms of staining or unevenness, the more you will have to sand away to achieve a good surface. For this reason, sand-ing is best carried out on solid wood floors. Veneered wood may not be thick enough to withstand such treatment.

Sanding is a job for the strong and fit. If you have any qualms about tackling the work, employ a specialist. It will add to the cost of the floor, but the overall expense will still be less than most new floor cov-erings and you will avoid the risk of either injuring yourself or irreparably damaging the floor. Alternatively, ask a friend who has successfully sanded a floor to help. If you are confident, the basic techniques of using a machine sander are shown on pages 168–69.

Decorative treatments and finishes

Most people who go to the bother of renovating old wood do so because they appreciate the inherent qualities of the raw material—the pattern of grain and warmth of tone. Others see a wood floor as a blank canvas for more decorative flights of fancy. Some want a bit of both worlds. All tastes can be catered to by adopting different finishing treatments.

If the "woodiness" of the floor is what appeals, you will want to finish it in such a way as to preserve those qualities, which generally means doing as little as possible to it. For a seamless look, you can fill gaps between planks with a mixture of wood glue or putty and sawdust, which will blend in with the basic tone and remain flexible enough to tolerate some movement. The floor will then simply need to be sealed to provide a water-resistant protective coat and make maintenance easier.

Any other finishing treatment needs to be carried out before the wood is sealed. Painted and decorated floors generally require up to five coats of protective varnish, which means that the area in question will be out of commission for a considerable period.

Bleaching and tinting

One of the simplest ways of altering the appearance of wooden floors is by bleaching or tinting to lighten or darken the basic tone.

Lightening the color of wood can transform an old floor into an elegant and pristine surface, more at ease with contemporary furnishings. Many old floors are made of pine, which has a warm honey color when sealed. In certain circumstances, however, sealed pine can look a little glaring and brash, an effect that certain types of sealant exacerbate, particularly those containing polyurethane, which tends to yellow with time. Bleaching knocks back the warmth of pine, even to the extent that it begins to resemble a more classy hardwood.

There are a number of different ways of lightening wood. Bleaching is the most extreme, as it takes almost all the color out of the wood. Another product which gives a similar effect is water-based white pigmented varnish, but it is very expensive.

Alternatively, wood can be lightened significantly by pickling. This effect is achieved by rubbing white into the grain of the wood. Any kind of white paint, proprietary pickling wax, or gesso can be used. Diluted white paint is best for pine. Oak is traditionally pickled by first darkening the wood with stain, pigment, or ammonia; the pickling sinks into the grain to give a weathered appearance. To achieve a pale pickled oak, the wood can be bleached first.

In some situations you may wish to deepen the natural tone of the wood. There are a number of tinted varnishes, wood dyes, and stains on the market in a choice of wood colors, from oak to mahogany, which give the wood a more seasoned look. These products can also be useful in spot applications, where a few original boards have been replaced with new wood. Normally, without such treatment, the new patches of flooring will stand out significantly from the rest. To distress new boards, apply a darker stain and then bleach slightly and stain again.

Above left: Whitewash and varnish have been used to lighten this staircase. Work into the grain with a wire brush before applying paint, pickling wax or gesso to ensure an even penetration.

Above center: A bleached oak floor creates a cool background in a hot climate. When applying bleach, it is important to work into the grain and along the boards, so that any discrepancies seem natural.

Above right: Pine boards can look quite stylish when stained and sealed. Apply stain to completely clean boards. For deeper, more saturated, color, you may need several coats.

Right: Pine has a rather orange tone when simply sanded and sealed, and the effect can be quite harsh. For subtler results, stain in another wood tone or color and finish with a flat varnish.

Color

The comprehensive selection of wood stains (dyes) and paints on
the market allows you to make a complete departure from the
natural wood palette without losing any of the other virtues of the
material itself.

Stain The real advantage of stain is that it soaks into the wood but
leaves the pattern of grain still in evidence. The trick is to make sure
to work evenly. Stains are available in a variety of forms: oil-, water-
or solvent-based. For the best results and the truest colors, it is best
to bleach the wood first so that you are starting out with as light a
background as possible. All stained floors must be sealed (see page
100) to make sure accidental spills do not soak into the wood,
showing as unsightly marks.

Paint is the answer if you want a solid, opaque color. Paintbox
primary colors make a splash in children's rooms and playrooms,
but painted floors can work equally well in different contexts beyond
the cheap and cheerful look. Pure white can be soothing and
sophisticated in an airy bedroom; black makes a dramatically
graphic foil for rugs. Changing the look of an entire room is straightforward enough, simply by painting over a different color or by
introducing another. Consider how long a room or area can be kept
out of commision, though, especially where using more than one
color, as you need to allow drying time between each coat.

**The opacity of paint is defining and unifying. Above: The soft green used
on the wood stairs has been used on the walls to suggest a baseboard.
Right: The duck-egg blue floor sets the style for the furnishing details.**

Although a variety of paints can be used on a wooden floor, not all paint is highly wear resistant, so it is best to restrict painted finishes to areas that are not subjected to a great deal of traffic. The final paint finish can be either oil-based gloss or eggshell (which has a sheen). Choose carefully: gloss has a shiny, reflective finish that can look chic or somewhat tacky, depending on the context. Egg-shell gives a softer, more subtle effect. No sealing is needed if you use gloss paint, but eggshell needs a coat of flat sealant for protection.

Special floor paints are available that contain epoxy resin or polyurethane for an extra hard finish, but the choice of colors may not be so broad as for gloss or eggshell. Yacht, or deck, paint makes an incredibly robust surface, but it is expensive, hard to apply, and takes longer to dry.

Pattern

If the sight of bare sanded boards arouses your decorative urges, there are potentially limitless ways of creating different patterns and effects. Many of the paint techniques that can be used to enliven walls will work equally well on floors—especially the bolder ones—from simple geometric patterning to fully realized trompe l'oeil. These effects can be used to add an element of richness and character or to provide a slightly tongue-in-cheek stand-in for a more expensive and luxurious surface. Some are definitely work for the professional; others are reasonably simple to achieve.

Broken-color techniques can be used to give depth and texture to a painted floor. The most successful are bold and forthright, such as spattering, combing, and graining; any discreet or subtle effect will be more or less lost underfoot. Stains or dyes are not suitable for these distressed or broken finishes; you need to use paint.

Spattering, as the term suggests, consists of flecking mineral spirits over still-wet color, which produces a pebblelike finish. The best effect is achieved by using two or more brightly contrasting shades, slapping down one color at a time, then scrabbling over the colors before they dry with a sponge to mix them roughly together.

Far left: The high glossused to paint the floorboards offsets the matte finish of the walls to create a chic all-white setting.

Left top: A "rug" painted on bare boards beside the bed provides an amusing—yet charming—decorative finish.

Left bottom: Paint effects do not have to be precise: the hand-drawn look can be effective, too.

Right: Subtle stenciling, in a hue slightly deeper than the natural tone of the wood, gives the impression of an inlaid floor.

Below left: Painting boards in two colors draws the eye away from a less than perfect surface.

Below: A precisely executed stencil over white painted boards echoes the colors and geometric pattern in the furnishing fabric.

Combing is similar to graining, but is more obvious and dramatic looking. The basic technique involves distressing a wet top coat with a comb to reveal patches of a different underlying color or hue. The result is a pattern of fine lines that gives a sense of movement and texture to the surface. Simple patterns often work best—either stripes or squares (rough accuracy rather than total precision is all part of the appeal). The choice of colors is very important. On the whole, combing is most successful when it combines different tones of the same basic shade. Spattering and combing techniques are illustrated on page 173.

Do not underestimate the time it takes to create a painted floor. You usually need to apply two base coats to undercoated wood and to allow drying time between each coat. When the paint is fully dry, several coats of polyurethane will give a very durable finish.

For painted floor patterns, the regular arrangement of the floorboards lends itself to creating allover geometric designs reminiscent of tiling. A checkerboard design can be executed simply enough, using the board widths as a basic dimensional template: one for small squares, two for medium size, and three for the largest scale. Paint or stain can be used to build up the design: paint gives a bold, crisp effect, while stain is more textural and muted. Good color contrasts include the classic black and white, ocher and terra-cotta, or terra-cotta and black.

Equally effective are patterns that echo the classic slab-and-keystone arrangement of traditional stone floors. Again, the basic geometry of the boards makes setting up the design much more straightforward. For more complex painted patterns, it is advisable to plan the design first on a scale plan of the floor drawn on graph paper (see page 170).

Borders

A painted border can also lift a plain floor out of the ordinary—and is a cheap and simple method of giving a made-to-order finish to a floor. It is a good paint effect to begin with, before tackling an all-over design. As with other types of flooring, setting in a border also provides a useful means of drawing the attention away from less-than-perfect proportions or any irregular features. The trick is to create a regular shape within the perimeter of the floor rather than slavishly follow the precise contours. Painting a border makes the floor look neat and finished, and adds just enough color contrast or pattern without being too fussy or insistent. It can also be used to define an area, such as the dining part of an open-plan room.

Stenciling

Stenciling is a good technique for decorative floor treatments, either in the form of borders, as edging for stairs, or as an allover pattern. The secret is to opt for crisp, definite designs scaled to suit the context. Small detailed patterns, especially as borders, can look halfhearted and rather ineffectual. Simple motifs, such as leaves, shells, fleur-de-lys, Greek key, and stars have greater impact. There are many precut stencil designs on the market or you can make your own using stencil board. Play up the contrast by stenciling in paint on a painted floor or opt for a subtler approach using stain on a stained ground or on natural wood. It may be wise to begin by stencilling a border before embarking on an entire floor.

Trompe l'oeil

More sophisticated decorative effects take the form of simulating another material, say marble, or, even more elaborately, creating a trompe l'oeil design. Truly convincing imitations are beyond the scope of all but the most artistic. Nevertheless, simplified versions of these techniques can score highly for bravado even if they are lacking in realism. A wood floor painted in a stylized marbled pattern will deceive no one, but has infinitely more character and flair than the same floor covered in marble-effect vinyl. The technique is achieved by simulating the cloudy translucency of the stone with layers of paint in closely related tones, with the characteristic veining and soft feathery lines painted on using an artist's brush while the top coat is still wet. Off-white marble is perhaps more convincingly imitated than the more strikingly colored varieties, but the principles are the same. Marbling is not an easy technique to master, so it would be as well to practice on a piece of board before tackling the floor itself.

Top and center top: A rural entranceway has been given a welcoming "mat", achieved by painting a background colour then stenciling on the design. The effect has been kept deliberately soft (see detail, center top), with the grain of the wood still apparent. The border of the "mat" has been carefully planned so that it neatly coincides with the edge of the boards themselves.

Above: The classic slab-and-keystone arrangement of traditional stone floors has been emulated in paint. The effect is fully in keeping with the grandeur and scale of the furnishings. This black-and-white treatment is a simple finish, but still needs to be well executed to be successful.

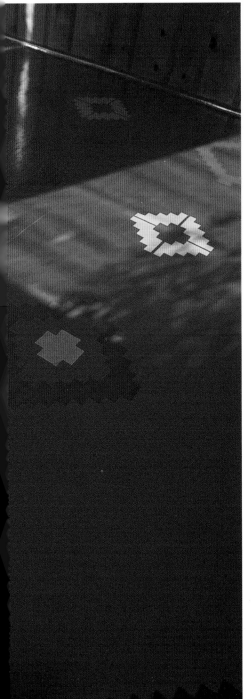

Above: Only a highly skilled artist could pull off such a sumptuously detailed trompe l'oeil as this "rug". It makes a fitting setting for defining a formal dining area.

Center: An allover treatment that saturates the underlying floorboards in vibrant color. Several coats of paint are required to achieve this solid effect. The spacing of the geometric motifs is appropriate for the generous proportions of the room.

Right: The geometric effect of marquetry (inlaid woodblocks of contrasting tones) is re-created in paint here. The result, achieved at a fraction of the cost of the real thing, suits the period decor of this apartment.

Sealing wood

Sealing is necessary for new, sanded, or decorated wood floors, with the exception of those that are pretreated or painted with gloss paint or floor or deck paint. Sealing protects the wood from water penetration and makes it resistant to dirt and chemical attack. Test the sealant before you apply it, because many alter the color of the wood and the effect varies according to the sealant and the type of wood. In addition, sealants are available in a number of different finishes, ranging from flat to high gloss, which will also affect the appearance of the finished floor.

Many types of hardwood flooring are supplied ready-sealed and need no further treatment and only minimal aftercare. Untreated wood may need to be sanded once it is laid, then finished with wax, polish, or oleoresinous sealant. Polyurethane varnish should not be applied until the wood has had a chance to acclimatize to the room where it is being laid; a period of up to twelve months is recommended—though this is not always practical.

Some sealants are hard-wearing and long-lasting; others may become scratched or stained and require more frequent renewal. Many commercial sealants contain polyurethane, which can cause allergies and skin and eye irritations when they are being applied. Wear gloves and eye protection when using these products. All sealants are highly flammable. If you are concerned about the use of chemicals in the home, you might consider traditional or natural alternatives based on resin and oil, or wax, although they do not offer such durability.

When applying solvent-based sealants, always keep windows open and the room well aired. It is also a good idea to wear a full face mask which will protect your eyes, nose and throat. Some sealants have a long curing time—up to 48 hours between coats—before the floor is ready to be walked on. The number of coats required will depend on the product and whether or not the floor has been painted or decorated. You also need to consider how heavily the floor is used. Kitchen floors, which usually have to withstand the most punishment of all, will need extra sealing, while up to five coats may be needed to protect a painted floor, three for a stained one. Sand lightly using fine-grit sandpaper between coats for the best results, and apply evenly, following the direction of the grain, using a wide natural bristle brush.

Types of sealant include:

Acrylic This is a water-soluble varnish, which is quick drying, non-toxic. It is also easy to apply. It needs to be waxed two to four times a year for additional protection.

Alkyd resin A nonyellowing, nontoxic, and quick-drying sealant. Like acrylic, it needs to be waxed two to four times a year for additional protection.

Button polish (shellac) This is the traditional floor sealant, but it is brittle and easily scratched and stained.

Epoxy resin This sealant is yellowish in tone, and slow to dry, but it is very hard wearing.

Natural sealants These are safe, environment-friendly products composed of resin and oil. Some include wax. They are water resistant and can be tinted with natural stains or colors.

Below left: Pine tends to look harshly orange when sealed with polyurethane. Bleaching the wood first can offset the tendency.

Below: Try out different sealants on offcuts and judge the effect in the room you intend to seal, before tackling the whole floor.

Below right and far right: Any wood floors that are likely to see spills of water, such as a garden room or kitchen, must be treated with several coats of sealant. Heavily used areas will likewise need several coats—and may still need renewing fairly regularly.

Oleoresinous These varnishes are a mixture of tung oil and resin (usually phenolic resin). They are clear but with a slight yellowish tinge and are slow drying but simple to apply. They are not the most hard wearing of sealants but are easy to patch.

Polyurethane This is one of the most common types of sealant. It brings out the yellow tones of wood and may also yellow with age. Polyurethane-based sealant is hard wearing but can cause irritation when applied. It is easy to patch.

Urea formaldehyde These transparent lacquers are ideal for light-colored or bleached woods. They are hard wearing, but difficult to patch repair.

Wax Special natural floor wax, consisting of a mixture of bees and plant waxes. It is durable, water resistant, and has a pleasant scent and antistatic properties. Liquid beeswax is also available.

Maintaining wood

Properly sealed and finished wood is easy to keep clean on a week-by-week basis. Vacuum or sweep up loose dirt regularly and wipe the floor with a damp cloth or a mop. Avoid wetting the floor too much and mop up spills as they occur. Use a mild detergent on stubborn marks if necessary.

If you have a waxed finish, the wax polish will need to be renewed at intervals—say every couple of months. Most sealants will last far longer. Areas of heavy traffic may wear out faster, but certain sealants, such as polyurethane, can be patch-repaired with ease. Use cups under the feet of furniture, and never drag heavy objects over the floor. Avoid spike heels at all costs—even at the risk of embarrassing your guests!

Sheet & Sof

Tiling

Sheet and its close associate, soft tiling, are the great cover-ups of the flooring world. This is not to imply that they hide a multitude of sins—no floor treatment will look or perform its best over a shoddy base—but they do provide a simple, quick, and relatively cheap way of creating a seamless or integrated effect while delivering maximum convenience.

Often, the distinction between tiling and sheet flooring is more practical than visual: tiles can be abutted without obvious seams while sheet flooring can be patterned to resemble tiles. Many different materials are now available in these two basic formats.

There are natural or near-natural types, such as linoleum, cork, and some forms of rubber. Others, vinyl, for instance, are just about as synthetic as you can get. The cost varies considerably. Linoleum, rubber, and top-quality vinyl are at the upper end of the scale and can be as expensive as the best carpet; cork is significantly cheaper. Quality also affects performance: linoleum lasts for years; cheap vinyl has a short life. Installation, too, varies across the board: laying soft tiles is the type of job any reasonably competent person could tackle in an afternoon (see pages 176–77), while putting down heavier sheet flooring over a large area is work requiring a skilled professional.

All these forms of tile and sheet have certain common attributes. They tend to be soft, warm, and comfortable underfoot, with the cushioned varieties providing a high degree of give. They are also lightweight, so you don't need to worry about the load-bearing capacity of a particular floor.

By and large, most of these materials lack the intense beauty that is the hallmark of more authentic types of flooring, such as stone and solid wood—although some people get distinctly emotional about linoleum. (Leather, of course, is in a class of its own.) Attractive and appropriate rather than irresistible, sheet and soft

tiling score highly for ease of maintenance and sheer practicality. With the exception of cork, these materials come in a staggering choice of colors, patterns, and textures. Sheet linoleum, in particular, offers great scope for custom designs. The mainstream market, however, tends to be dominated by designs that simulate other, more innately soulful materials, with countless variations on wood, stone, marble, quarry and brick effects.

The whole issue of simulated flooring has a tendency to bring out the style police in full force. The less convincing simulations do have a rather apologetic, cringing quality that many people find depressing. Yet at the same time, really skillful vinyl copies (which can be quite expensive) have their own built-in letdown. Ultimately, no matter how visually close such simulations are to reality, the fact that they can never sound, smell, or feel like the real thing will inevitably give the game away. With time, this perception will only become more acute. Synthetic flooring does not wear like its natural counterpart. Its pristine perfection when new lacks the random depth of character of materials such as wood and stone, and once it begins to degrade, it tends to lose charm completely.

That said, some simulations do eventually acquire an odd sort of "rightness" just through prevalence, while others may be prized by devotees of kitsch. In terms of style, though, it can often be a better idea to choose a synthetic floor with a design that displays an abstraction of pattern or that summarizes the qualities of another material rather than one that is an outright pastiche. Marbleized tiles, for example, have the cloudy, veined pattern of the stone in graphic form without attempting to provide a complete replica of it. There are also plenty of exciting colors, patterns, and finishes that are not trying to be something else and are all the better for it. It is, however, unrealistic to imagine you can deceive anyone for long into believing that they are walking across oak parquet when they are in fact treading on a clever vinyl look-alike. But for those who wish to take the appearance of a natural floor into areas such as kitchens, where maintenance would otherwise be prohibitively demanding, a good simulation may do the trick.

Although this family of flooring materials may essentially comprise workhorses rather than thoroughbreds, style police dictates or no, there will always be room for them somewhere in the home at some stage in life. Undoubtedly, many of these materials are chosen as a stopgap or as a sensible solution for hardworking utility areas, but there is no reason why they should not be viewed more positively. Where they are employed with confidence and flair, the style dividends can be as high as the practical benefits.

Left: Employed with wit and flair, practical flooring such as linoleum can pay handsome style dividends. Vibrant color, bold pattern, and contrasting borders are combined here for maximum impact.

Cork

Soft, quiet, and comfortable, cork makes a good-looking practical floor in many areas of the home. Derived from the bark of the cork oak (*Quercus suber*), an evergreen native to Mediterranean areas, its warm neutral tones and open texture have a sympathetically natural appearance. Cork oak is grown commercially for the purpose of extracting the bark—a process that does no harm to the tree, which simply regenerates it. The cork bark is then granulated, pressed with binders such as resins, and baked.

Anyone who has ever pulled a cork from a bottle and seen it spring back into shape can appreciate the remarkable resilience of this material. It is this quality that makes cork extremely comfortable to stand on and walk across, reasonably resistant to indentation from heels or furniture legs, and quiet, too—valuable attributes for use in children's rooms and playrooms, kitchens, bathrooms, and halls. In all these respects, cork scores more highly than linoleum. It is also antistatic and nonslip, even when it is wet or polished.

Cork can be used unsealed in the bathroom, where the effect is similar to having a large absorbent bathmat permanently in situ, but normally it does need sealing to prevent dirt from becoming ingrained. In areas of high traffic, such as around the kitchen sink or by the front door, cork can look shabby rather quickly, and for

Above: Warm and quiet, cork makes a practical floor for dining areas, as it is easy to keep clean and will not amplify the sounds of chairs scraping across the floor.

Left: Contemporary, but lacking the hard edge of more industrial materials, cork's mellow honey tones complement the clean lines of a modern study-bedroom. The blinds help to screen strong sunlight which will cause cork to fade slightly.

this reason it has acquired a rather drab image in some people's minds. However, with appropriate use and treatment, a cork floor can maintain its handsome and unpretentious appearance.

Most cork is sold in the natural shades of pale honey to dark brown, but there are colored versions, including charcoal, green, and blue. Using contrasting colors or an inset border will add an extra element of style. Tiles (sealed or unsealed) are the standard format, and the thicker the tile, the more hard-wearing the floor will be. Cork wall tiles are not suitable; the cork must be flooring grade. Cork sheet or "carpet" with a jute canvas backing is also available, but it is more unwieldy to install. Some manufacturers produce composite cork flooring, which offers much greater wear resistance and durability, but at the expense of a slight compromise of the natural qualities of cork. Such flooring consists of a layer of

compressed cork sandwiched between a vinyl backing and a cork finish or veneer, sealed with a layer of clear vinyl. It is available in tile or plank form and in a wider choice of colors. There is also veneered tongue-and-groove strip flooring, with cork substituting for wood as the final finish over compressed cork, composite board, and a plywood base.

Laying

Natural cork tiles are lightweight and easy to cut and lay. They require a dry, level subfloor, such as floorboards covered with a layer of masonite or plywood. Paper felt laid over the masonite will prevent any nail heads from working through. Concrete subfloors at ground level need a dampproof membrane. Cork cannot be laid over underfloor heating, which would cause the tiles to lift. To allow the material to adjust to the ambient temperature, the tiles need to be stored in the room in which they will be laid for 48 hours before gluing with the recommended adhesive. (Organic adhesives can be used.) Planks should also be glued. No expansion gaps are necessary around the perimeter of the room. Tiles may need to be weighted until the adhesive has set.

Cork-veneered strip flooring can be laid as a floating floor, without nailing or gluing the strips to the underlying surface. The advantage is that the strip floor can be taken up at a later date without

Far left: Cork remains nonslip, even when it becomes wet, a quality that makes it eminently suitable for bathrooms. A contrasting border has been used to define the cork wall tiling around the bathtub and create a tiled effect on the floor.

Left: Sealing is recommended to prolong the life of cork flooring which can be damaged by grit. Even presealed tiles benefit from an extra coat to ensure the joints are fully waterproof.

affecting the existing floor beneath. The tongue-and-groove planks are slotted together, with a PVA adhesive used along the tongue to seal the floor against dust. An expansion gap of ¼ to ½ inch is needed around the perimeter of the room.

Sealing and maintenance

Sealing is strongly recommended to protect the cork from soiling and to make it water resistant. After laying, allow about 48 hours before sealing to give the adhesive time to cure. Three or four coats of polyurethane or polymer sealant will prevent the surface from degrading: allow adequate time between each coat. Presealed cork can be given a single extra coat of sealant after laying to prevent moisture from penetrating joints. Alternatively, unsealed cork can be polished with wax or dressed with organic primers. Cork flooring that has a vinyl finish needs no subsequent treatment.

Despite being economic and straightforward to lay, a cork floor demands dedicated upkeep to preserve its appearance. It is important to make sure the cork is kept clean and free from grit, which might break down the seal and allow dirt and moisture through. Sweep or vacuum regularly, wipe with a damp cloth, and polish occasionally and sparingly.

Rubber

With its tough industrial aesthetic, rubber flooring has long been a favorite with modern architects and designers. Widely used in train stations, airports, and other public transit areas (even on spacecraft), studded or embossed rubber migrated to the home with the arrival of high-tech in the late 1970s. High-tech, as a trend, did not last long, but rubber flooring is once again showing signs of a revival among those at the cutting edge of interior fashion, mainly because a wider choice of colors is now available.

You don't need to be in the stylistic vanguard to appreciate the considerable practical advantages of rubber as a household flooring material. Hardwearing, water and burn resistant, extremely resilient, quiet, and warm, it has all the qualities anyone would wish from a utility floor. Naturally, it is in bathrooms, kitchens, and other service areas that its use is most prevalent. Nevertheless, there is plenty of potential for a wider application.

Natural rubber is less consistent and harder to color than synthetic varieties, and most of the rubber now sold for use in flooring applications contains few if any natural elements. Instead it consists of vulcanized synthetic rubber, pigment, silica, and china clay. Some types also come with fabric or foam-rubber backing. Rubber is most commonly available in tile form, but wide rolls, stair

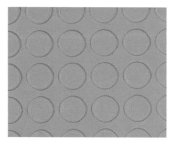

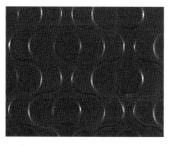

Right (details): Rubber flooring has shed some of its harder industrial aesthetic to be reborn in a wide choice of brilliant colors, abstract patterns and textural relief patterns. The textured versions add grip, and are recommended for stairs or areas which are likely to become wet, although the relief patterns tend to trap dirt and require more regular maintenance than the smooth finishes.

Left: Svelte and sophisticated, this jolt of lemon yellow makes a bold modern statement in a living area.

Right: Rich brown rubber flooring complements the cool blue-green kitchen decor. Rubber does stain, so extra care must be taken where spills are likely, and sealing is advisable.

Above and below right: Ideal for bathrooms with attitude, rubber flooring provides a depth of pure color. Rubber can become slippery when wet, however.

tiles, and runners are also produced. It varies in thickness, which affects the price. The best grades will cost you as much as top-quality vinyl or woodblock flooring.

In the first flush of enthusiasm for rubber flooring, black and gray were popular colors, accentuating the severe high-tech look, with the occasional brilliant blue, grass green, and scorching yellow making a more vivid statement. Nowadays, rubber flooring comes in a vast range of colors, from bright paintbox primaries to soft, subtle tones that lack any hint of the factory floor. There is an equivalent variety of finishes and patterns. In addition to smooth, matte solid colors, there are various raised textures including round studs, ribs, grooves, and designs reminiscent of metal tread, that are intended to improve grip, and broken color effects such as marbling, striation, and flecking designed to disguise dirt.

Studded rubber is a good choice for any area likely to become wet — smooth finishes can become very slippery. Dirt and food spills have tendency to accumulate around relief patterns, however, and extra maintenance may be needed to keep the floor clean. Unpolished matte rubber marks easily. There is a special grade available for laying over underfloor heating, but the warmth may bring out a rubbery smell.

Rubber flooring is often laid as a single-color floor, but tiles can be bought in contrasting shades to make a checkerboard effect or in a more random medley of colors. Sheet rubber lends itself to the same sort of cut patterns as sheet linoleum.

Laying
Rubber is supple, easy to cut and shape, and lasts forever. It must be laid over a dry, flat subfloor — either floorboards covered with masonite or plywood, or concrete. Solid floors at ground level may need a dampproof membrane. Both tiles and sheet need to be bonded to the subfloor with adhesive. Recommended rubber adhesives are usually applied both to the subfloor and the flooring, and the two surfaces brought together after a specified period. After laying, allow about 48 hours before polishing to give the adhesive time to cure.

Maintenance
Tiles may come with a surface layer of dust which has to be removed with a special cleaner. Rubber can be left matte for a warm, soft look or polished with a water-soluble wax emulsion. Natural rubber is readily marked by fats and solvents, but even synthetic rubber can be damaged if left unpolished. Use polish sparingly and renew it from time to time.

Left: Gray rubber flooring makes a good foil for the other rich spice colors used in this uncompromisingly modern setting.

Below: Rubber can be polished with a water-soluble wax emulsion. Waxing intensifies its color and increases stain resistance, which is important in kitchens and dining areas.

Bottom: The usual purity and simplicity often associated with bathroom decor has been cheerfully ignored in this checkerboard design of colored rubber floor tiles.

Linoleum

Linoleum is the Cinderella of flooring materials. In the not-too-distant past, it was fairly universally reviled as the grim, cracked utility covering of old hospital corridors, but in recent years, manufacturers have virtually reinvented the product, transforming a brittle and often lurid material into a sleek, robust flooring available in a huge selection of colors and patterns. This reincarnation has coincided with increased public awareness of environmental issues. Linoleum is a wholly natural product that just happens to deliver many of the same practical advantages of similar synthetic types of flooring, along with other benefits uniquely its own.

Linoleum has had a respectable history since its invention in 1863 by the Englishman Frederick Walton. It grew in popularity from the latter decades of the 19th century when it was first put into mass production, serving as a cheap, practical, and more durable

Right: Linoleum has a naturally mottled appearance which softens the effect of graphic patterning, such as this simple checked floor. Tiles are easier to install than sheet linoleum.

Below: Borders and central motifs lift linoleum out of the ordinary. Practically speaking, linoleum makes an excellent kitchen floor, being naturally antibacterial and easy to maintain.

Above: Linoleum is now available in a choice of exciting new colors and designs, transforming its image from workaday practicality into a sleek, stylish contemporary material.

alternative to oilcloth. It proved exceptionally durable; examples of old linoleum floors dating back to the early decades of the 20th century are still discovered from time to time in out-of-the-way buildings. Linoleum was often printed in designs that reflected the style of the period; Bauhaus architects were fascinated by the material, and some, including Mies van der Rohe, Behrens, and Hoffman, produced designs for it.

Earlier forms of linoleum were, however, brittle in comparison to today's versions, and dreary cracked tiles or sheet curling at the edges helped to give the flooring a depressing, second-rate image. The image problem was not helped by the misleadingly termed "printed linoleums," cheap ersatz products of very poor quality which were essentially painted bituminous felt. The introduction of vinyl flooring after World War II marked the beginning of the long decline of linoleum in its popularity.

of finishes, including marbled, streaked, striated, flecked, and mottled. Colors range from intense hues to pale tones, but all have a natural, slightly soft quality. New designs include geometric patterns, such as plaid, gingham, keystone, and box (or tumbling block), as well as a selection of borders. The latest technology has revolutionized the creation of inlaid designs: very complicated patterns and well-defined motifs can be realized by computer-controlled precision cutting.

Linoleum is damaged by moisture; careful laying is important to prevent water from penetrating seams and rotting the floor from below. Sheet linoleum can be hot-seam welded to make it watertight; tiles must be abutted tightly. While the material itself is not exorbitantly expensive, the cost of professional laying can push the price of a finished floor into the upper bracket, particularly in the case of an inlaid design. Tiles can be laid by skilled amateurs, but sheet linoleum is heavy and unwieldy, and needs expert attention. Once laid, although it is proof against most household chemicals, linoleum can be damaged by a variety of solvents.

Like most natural products, linoleum improves with age. The linseed oil used in its manufacture continues to mature for up to ten years, which means that it actually gets tougher as time goes by.

One particular feature of linoleum is what is known as "stove yellowing," a temporary discoloration that arises as part of the maturing process of the material in the ovens. It is especially noticeable on white, blue, or gray shades as a yellow tint or oxidation film, but it disappears within a few hours when the material is exposed to sunlight. In dark areas, such as basements, the tint may last for up to several weeks. The effect may be particularly apparent when comparing a section of laid floor with unlaid linoleum from the same batch, but does not reflect discrepancies in the material itself.

Linoleum needs a period of acclimatization before laying, up to 48 hours at room temperature. Tiles should be laid butted up tightly against each other. Seams have a tendency to get tighter with age, rather than to shrink, which helps prevent moisture from getting through. Linoleum in sheet form is generally available in 2-yard widths. It is heavy and not as pliable as vinyl or rubber, which makes installation a job for a professional. In sheet or tile form, linoleum must be glued in place with emulsion, synthetic rubber resin, or powder adhesive. Sheet linoleum should be firmly flattened with a floor roller and any seams hot-seam welded.

The contemporary revival reflects technical improvements that have greatly increased the scope of color, pattern, and design. At the same time, attention has been focused on the many other estimable qualities of linoleum. It is not only a natural product, but a healthy one. It is antistatic, which means it does not attract dust and house mites, which can trigger asthma or allergenic reactions. Equally important, linoleum is antibacterial, naturally killing off germs that come into contact with it, an asset that has long made it a popular choice for hospital flooring. It is warm, quiet, resilient, comfortable to walk on, and reasonably nonslip even when wet. All of these qualities are enhanced in the thicker, more expensive grades. There are special varieties, such as cork-backed linoleum, which give a high degree of cushioning and sound absorption, and hardened grades, which are very resistant to indentation and burns. All types can be used over underfloor heating.

Linoleum takes its name from *Oleum lini*, the linseed oil derived from flax. To make linoleum, linseed oil is oxidized and natural pine resin (rosin) is added as a hardener. The linoleum "cement" is then mixed with powdered cork, which provides its insulating qualities and flexibility, and wood flour and powdered limestone, which lend hardness and strength. Pigments are added for color. The raw material is then pressed onto a woven jute or burlap backing and left for several weeks in a drying chamber, where it is baked at high temperatures. It is then ready to be cut into rolls.

Linoleum has a naturally grainy matte finish, which can be buffed and polished to a glossy sheen. It is available in an enormous choice of color, twice as many in sheet as in tile, as well as a variety

Inlaid patterns

Original designs are made by cutting and piecing sections of sheet linoleum or by inlaying a decorative border. The cut elements are then supplied ready to install by a professional floor layer: the end results can elevate a linoleum floor from a position backstage into one that well deserves the limelight. Many manufacturers offer a custom service for the commissioning of individual patterns. The price will vary according to the complexity and detail of the design and the number of colors employed. In the past, creating an inlaid design depended exclusively on the craft skills of the floor layer. Nowadays, designs are fed into a computer that controls the cutting of the inlaid pattern with high-pressure water jets. Inlaid patterns range from simple curved contours, pathways, and random insets to the more complex and detailed designs facilitated by precision cutting.

Installation is an operation that requires great skill. The background linoleum is first dry-laid on the floor and the inlays placed on top and marked accurately in position. Then the background is removed and the inlays are stuck into their measured positions and rolled and weighted if necessary. Finally, the background is cut so that it overlaps the inlay slightly, stuck down in place, and trimmed to fit. Any small gaps can be filled and polished with linoleum dust blended with diluted emulsion.

Laying

Linoleum should be laid over a dry, flat subfloor, such as floorboards covered with masonite, plywood, or concrete. Concrete at ground level needs a damp proof membrane. The thicker grades of linoleum will make up for slight imperfections in the base, but unevenness needs to be remedied because it may cause the linoleum to crack.

Above: Sheet linoleum in a fresh gingham check works well in a traditional kitchen.

Right: The matte tones of sheet linoleum in a solid color make a good foil for a modern kitchen.

Below left: Following the contours of built-in features, a border inset in sheet linoleum adds a sense of definition.

Below right: Dramatically glossy, highly polished black linoleum makes an Art Deco background.

Far right: Linoleum has a pleasing grainy matte texture with a slightly soft quality. It comes in a huge choice of colors and finishes.

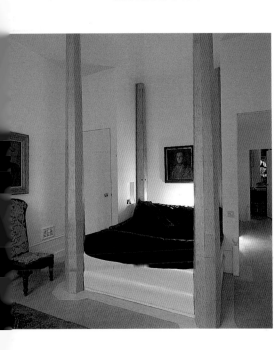

Vinyl

Vinyl is the term given to a range of synthetic flooring products that contain some proportion of polyvinyl chloride (PVC). First developed in the 1950s, PVC is a thermoplastic, in other words, a type of plastic that retains the ability to be softened by heat, a characteristic that gives it flexibility. The actual amount of PVC in vinyl tiles and sheet varies; the higher the percentage, the better the performance and quality and the higher the price.

Vinyl is very popular mainstream flooring. Affordable, easy to install, nonallergenic, simple to maintain, and with a reasonable lifespan, it offers a straightforward and practical solution to many flooring needs. The choice of colors, patterns, textures, and effects on the market is huge. Vinyl is available in a choice of thicknesses and tile sizes and standard sheet widths of 6, 10, and 12 feet, which makes it possible to cover most floors seamlessly.

Above: At the top end of the market, vinyl is available in some very convincing simulations, such as this marble look-alike.

Above right: Neutral, economical, and durable, vinyl in a simple textural pattern makes easy-care kitchen flooring.

Right and center right: Black and white is a classic format, good-looking enough for either living areas or kitchen. Suit the scale of the tile to the area in question.

Far right: Textured vinyl makes a vivid nonslip covering for stairs.

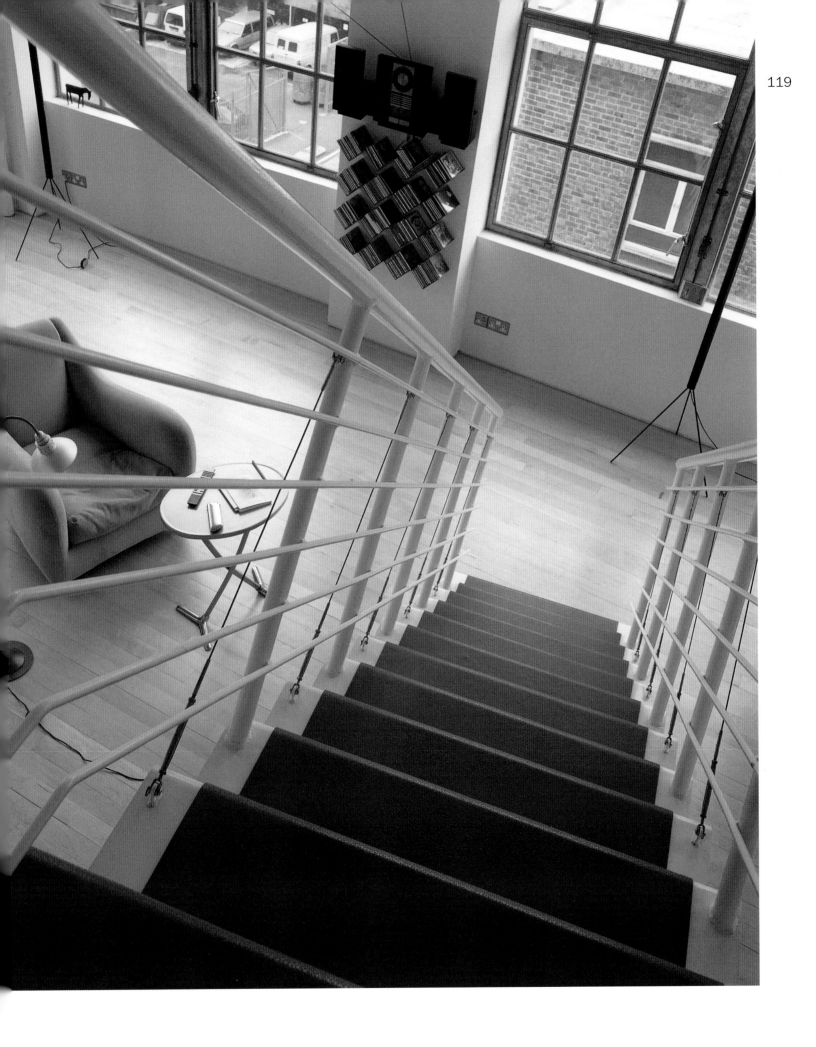

Practicality is a major selling point. Vinyl is waterproof, resists oils, fats, and most household chemicals, and makes an easy-care, all-purpose flooring. Cushioned vinyl, which has an interlayer of foam, and vinyl backed with foam rubber provide extra resilience and better sound and heat insulation. Vinyl can be used over underfloor heating and sometimes laid directly over existing floor coverings.

As far as appearance is concerned, simulations of natural materials dominate the quality end of the market. In fact, in the literature of some manufacturers, it can be difficult to find any mention of the synthetic origins of the product at all, with coy terminology such as "marble design" or "beech effect" hinting at more worthy antecedents. Many of these simulations are very

Left: A simple centered motif, reminiscent of a scatter rug, provides interest on a landing covered with sheet vinyl.

Below: Bright colors and speckles or streaks are vinyl's strong suit.

Left: Suggestive of the slightly marbled effect of linoleum, the textural quality of this vinyl floor provides interest and character in the absence of strong color. Vinyl does not require sealing, but it can be damaged prematurely by the use of abrasive cleaners, which will cause discoloration.

highly realized, with shading, graining, and textural variations faithfully rendered. Vinyl wood-effect flooring even comes in random "planks." Popular simulations include all forms of wood, from hardwood parquet to rustic boards, as well as the ever-popular marble, slate, brick, quarry tile, and terrazzo. The vinyl versions, unlike the natural materials they mimic, can be readily combined in the same floor or as borders. Custom-design services are available from leading manufacturers, with computer realizations offering a preview of the final effect, as well as an installation plan and a cutting list to make laying simpler.

Such high-level simulations do not come cheap, although in comparison with nonsynthetic materials, the price is much more favorable once the cost of laying and maintaining the floor has been taken into account. It is important to remember, however, that what may look utterly convincing in a full-color brochure will inevitably lack some degree of authenticity in real life. Marble-effect vinyl, for example, is warm to the touch; beech-effect vinyl will never acquire more patina than what it has in simulated form already: the beauty is literally only skin deep. To some people the whole concept of simulated materials is anathema; others relish the opportunity to live with the appearance of a natural floor without the bother of looking after it.

Simulated designs are not the only types available. There are simple geometric patterns that can look very clean and fresh; mottled, speckled, metallic, and flecked finishes; and lively contemporary styles. Particularly striking are those vinyls that achieve an almost three-dimensional effect by suspending colored plastic granules or glittering quartz flakes under a clear surface layer — similar to industrial or contract vinyls that use chips or fragments of natural fillers to increase slip resistance (smooth

vinyl is slippery when wet). Such designs sparkle as they catch the light in different directions; one style even glows in the dark. The whole notion of simulated flooring has been given an original, witty twist by one designer who has come up with the idea of photographic tiles. Protected by a durable vinyl coating and backed by cork, the tiles show shots of outdoor landscapes at close quarters: a pattern of waves; a sandy beach complete with shells; rocks and pebbles; and wildflowers — ideal for creating a watery bathroom floor or rocky entrance.

For anyone who relishes the cheap and cheerful look of plastic, there are also PVC runners and mats. These temporary cover-ups come in a range of colors and "weaves," as well as in more sophisticated neutral shades and rougher textures, that have the look of natural fiber matting.

Despite its reputation for practicality, vinyl does have some disadvantages. The quality of the subfloor matters a great deal: many types of vinyl are not thick enough to absorb minor discrepancies, and underlying ridges, bumps, or protruding nail heads will show up on the surface, where they may cause patches of wear or even holes.

Any sign of wear has an entirely negative effect on appearance and performance. Unlike natural materials, which may mellow with time, worn vinyl is merely shoddy. For this reason, you must make sure that the right cleaning products are used and that the floor is protected from grit and the type of mars and spills most likely to damage it. Black rubber heel marks can be particularly detrimental; if not tackled immediately, antioxidants in the rubber can stain permanently. Rubber-backed rugs and mats can cause similar problems. Vinyl is badly damaged by cigarette burns.

Finally, vinyl is not a material for anyone concerned about environmental issues. Soft plastics such as PVC have been identified as among those most likely to "offgas," or release potentially hazardous chemicals into the atmosphere. If vinyl catches fire, the fumes are toxic. The manufacture of vinyl also consumes nonrenewable resources of petroleum and natural gas, and the product itself is not biodegradable.

Laying
see pages 176–77.

Maintenance
Vinyl requires no sealing, but you must follow correct maintenance procedures to prevent the material from becoming worn too quickly. The surface can be torn by dragging heavy items over it and premature damage caused by the use of the wrong cleaners. See pages 180–81 for advice on its upkeep.

Leather

Utterly sublime, extravagant, and expensive, leather tiles are the height of sophistication. For the home that has everything — and the homeowner with deep pockets — leather makes an unusual and truly classy floor, bursting with warmth and character. It naturally works well in the cozy atmosphere of a study or library, but also in contemporary living spaces with clean, modern lines.

The tiles are made of steer hide cut from the center portion, which has the toughest fibers, cured by traditional vegetable tanning, and dyed with aniline dyes. Colors include natural, dark red, rust, brown, dark green, and black; and the finish can be either smooth or antique textured to resemble boar hide. Sizes and shapes of tiles differ, so a variety of patterns can be created.

Leather is warm, comfortable, resilient, sound absorbent, and durable; underfoot it feels and sounds a little like walking across a wooden floor. Like other natural materials, it improves with age and use, acquiring a deep, rich patina with repeated waxing and buffing. It is, however, far from a utility covering and should not be laid in kitchens or bathrooms. The price is in the upper range, comparable to natural stone or the best quality ceramic tile.

Opposite: In a Japanese-inspired interior, leather flooring provides a material sensuality to complement the translucent rice-paper screens and wood detailing.

Top right and near right: For a look of understated luxury, nothing is more effective than leather. Restricting the decor in a warm palette of neutral shades, from honey to biscuit, keeps the look chic and classy.

Far right: Leather can be dyed in a range of rich colors, such as this intense red. Repeated waxing will produce a high gloss and protect the surface from damage.

Leather should be laid on a dry, even base, preferably on masonite or plywood. It is bonded with contact adhesive. The tiles should be laid to a straight line (since perimeters are rarely absolutely parallel) and abutted closely together. Slight variations may also occur in tile size and shape, and any gaps can be filled with carnuba wax, which will act as a grout.

Waxing provides basic moisture resistance, and spills, if tackled immediately, will wipe off. Scratches are inevitable but add to the character; a well-used floor has great depth of appeal.

Soft floors

Carpet, rugs, and natural fiber coverings occupy the "soft" end of the flooring spectrum. These materials tend to be warm, comfortable, quiet, and enclosing—as well as fairly impractical for hardworking utility areas such as bathrooms and kitchens. In almost every other respect, however, generalizations are largely meaningless: price, composition, performance, color, pattern, and texture vary widely.

Wall-to-wall carpeting is synonymous with the modern lifestyle. Along with central heating and open-plan spatial arrangements, fully carpeted rooms became a signature of a certain kind of postwar interior—informal and, above all, comfortable. What was once so progressive can, however, seem a little passé. Like other furnishings that were status symbols a few decades ago, carpeting has lost some of its former glamour. Its appeal has never waned for use in bedrooms, but carpet is now less of an instinctive choice for living areas, losing ground in style-conscious circles to wood and natural-fiber coverings. In recognition of the shift in popularity, some manufacturers are now producing wool carpet in sisal-look weaves to give a classic product a more updated image.

The runaway flooring success of recent years, natural fiber, encompasses a range of materials from bristly coir to the smooth sophistication of woven jute. With their natural credentials and

Loose-laid rugs are a study in themselves, from the priceless Persian with its tribal iconography to the cheap machine-washable cotton dhurrie. Rugs may seem accessories of the flooring world, offering instant uplift, warmth, color, comfort, and drama, but they are often much more than a mere accent or finishing touch. A beautiful rug can be the centerpiece of the entire room, its colors and design forming the foundation for the decorative scheme.

With the exception of rugs, most soft floors benefit from professional laying. At the cheaper end of the market, foam-backed carpet can be laid by an amateur (see pages 178–79), but most carpeting and natural-fiber floorings are as unwieldy as sheet flooring and demand expertise to fit. Also, most types of soft flooring stain easily, and, while stain-inhibiting treatments are available, you need to be more vigilant to make sure they retain their good looks.

Soft flooring appeals to our sensual nature, inviting us to kick off our shoes and lounge on the floor. A home fitted with carpet from the front door to the attic steps might be a deadened, overly cushioned place (and indeed an impractical one), yet a home without any soft surfaces would be unyielding, rackety, and harsh. Textile or woven coverings offer the opportunity to change the pace and the mood.

Left: New custom designs extend the scope of carpet pattern into exciting dimensions. Random or abstract designs marry particularly well with the modern aesthetic. There are now a number of high-quality manufacturers who will produce carpets and rugs to original specifications.

Right: The work of a Finnish designer, these luminous soft floor coverings are made from paper twine.

Far right: Natural-fiber coverings make a great base for loose-laid rugs.

historic pedigrees, these types of soft flooring satisfy the contemporary desire for authenticity on both counts. Although stronger shades are increasingly featured, a pleasing neutrality is the norm, a muted palette that is given depth by the texture of both weaves and fibers, albeit at the expense of a slight compromise in comfort. Manufacturers and suppliers are rapidly extending the choice of colors and patterns, as well as improving practical performance of natural fiber coverings.

Above: Contemporary rug design is a flourishing field. The work of classic modern designers such as Eileen Gray is still in production, along with many innovative designs by newer talents.

Below: Runners are a sympathetic complement to the country-house look. Vibrant colors are set off with pristine white woodwork.

Carpet

Carpet conveys a sense of warmth, intimacy, and comfort which many find irresistible—and it is one of the most popular of all flooring options. Although it has become a much more predictable and immediate choice for the average homeowner over the last few decades, it still evokes a feeling of luxuriousness and indulgence. Carpet is the softest flooring material available and positively encourages the most direct contact—whether it is bare feet getting out of bed in the morning, bare young knees crawling around on the floor, or simply the easy informality of wandering around the house without shoes.

Carpet did not become a term applied to floor coverings until the mid-18th century, when the first carpet factories were established in continental Europe and Britain, making widths that could be pieced or sewn together to cover an entire floor. Early English manufactures included Wilton, in Wiltshire, founded around 1740, which made carpet with a cut-pile surface, while other factories, notably at Kidderminster in Worcestershire, made so-called in-grain, or Scotch, carpet, a flat-weave variety with no pile. Carpet—in the sense of a large unfitted covering with a pile surface woven in a single piece—also began to be made in the West at this time, notably in France, at the Savonnerie factory near Paris, and in south-western England, at the Axminster factory. These carpets were luxurious and expensive, much more costly than the Oriental or Turkish versions. (For the purposes of this chapter, the term *carpet* is used in the modern sense to refer to an integral wall-to-wall covering, rather than the type of unfitted carpet sometimes known as an "area rug.")

As the pace of industrialization accelerated throughout the 19th century, technical innovations on both sides of the Atlantic allowed carpets to be produced in more complex designs and in greater volumes to reach a wider market. A similar watershed occurred after World War II, with the advent of synthetic fibers and tufted carpet construction.

Far left: Carpet tends to create a sense of enclosure, which is good for unifying spaces.

Left: Soft, warm, and comfortable, carpet accentuates the soothing intimacy of an all-white bedroom.

Below: Hard materials can be noisy on stairs, and carpet often makes a more practical solution. This elegant herringbone design with contrast banding adds a graphic edge. Stair carpeting can also be loose-laid, secured firmly in place with stair rods, which means the carpet can be turned periodically to even out wear.

Right: The textural quality of this weave adds character and visual interest when colors are muted and natural.

Far right: A specially commissioned carpet in pale oatmeal cord makes a suitably discreet partner for the light, airy decorations.

In the modern home, fitted carpet provides a fail-safe way to increase the sense of space where proportions are cramped or limited. Running the same carpet throughout a number of different rooms and adjoining areas has a seamless, coordinated effect, particularly if everything is on the same level. Alternatively, where space is not an issue, carpet can be very effective as a way of emphasizing a change of atmosphere. Carpeting in a bedroom, study, or living room underscores the difference between busy, public, or working areas and more relaxing private enclaves. In this respect, it can create a sense of enclosure rather than space.

Choosing carpet demands careful research. Carpets vary in just about every conceivable way, from composition, construction, and grade to color, pattern, and texture. All of these parameters will have an impact not only on appearance and performance but also on your budget. In general, it is always better to opt for the best quality you can afford; this is even more true of carpet than of other types of flooring. Cheap carpet wears incredibly badly and will need replacing within a short space of time, which may well entail extra expense in the long run. If you are looking for a bargain, it is better to search out suppliers specializing in room-size remnants, ends of rolls, or discontinued stock than to make a compromise on basic quality.

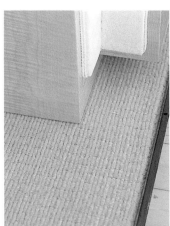

In terms of style and appearance, the choice of colors and designs offers virtually unlimited decorative potential. It is important to remember, however, that with any luck – and careful maintenance – a good carpet should last for many years and may have to work with successive wall colors or decorating schemes. On the other hand, plain neutral carpet may be safe but is unlikely to set pulses racing. The right carpet should offer some stylistic contribution of its own without setting unrealistic limits on what you can do with the room in the future.

Carpet styles tend to go in and out of fashion with more frequency than other types of flooring. One case in point is shag pile. The epitome of chic several decades ago, shag pile was subsequently cast aside as irredeemably downscale and suburban, only to be rediscovered, more recently, by knowing young converts to 1960s style. Charcoal-gray cord carpet enjoyed a long run of popularity among architects and designers who favored its no-nonsense neutrality, but sheer familiarity has inevitably dulled some of its hard-edged impact. Today, striped or muted flat weaves and tightly woven pale wool with cut-and-loop self-colored relief patterns are experiencing something of a vogue, in part in response to the contemporary interest in the natural look.

Above left: White is a challenging color in the home, demanding perfect upkeep and maintenance, but the decorative benefits can be equally high.

Top: A dark wood strip makes a neat edge between surfaces.

Above: Pleasing neutrality acts as a foil for strong architecture.

Right: Wall-to-wall carpeting in muted colors goes hand in hand with the contemporary look.

Practically speaking, there are various grades of carpet to suit most locations in the home, other than areas likely to get wet regularly. Carpet can be used in bathrooms; indeed, in many homes it has a luxurious and humanizing effect in what might otherwise be a cold and clinical room. But it is inadvisable to carpet a family bathroom, where spills and splashes are more common: carpet does not withstand repeated soaking and will eventually rot. Similarly, carpet does not represent a practical choice for kitchens, except for carpet tiles, whose aesthetic appeal leaves much to be desired.

Carpet, as a soft floor covering, is resilient and quiet as well as warm and comfortable. It muffles sound and cushions feet. Deep- or shag-pile carpets can, however, be surprisingly tiring because of their extreme softness, in the same way as walking on dry, shifting sand can be an effort.

Manufacturers have worked hard to counteract carpet's basic practical deficiency, which is its readiness to stain. Many carpets have a protective finish or can be treated to make them easier to maintain on a daily basis. However, there is no avoiding the fact that carpet does stain and demands a certain degree of vigilance to remain in good condition. Familiarity with stain-removal techniques is useful, and it is a good idea to keep supplies of solvents and cleaners on hand for emergencies. Some people choose to solve the problem by opting for a hectic or busy pattern in the hope that it will not show dirt or stains; such designs do provide basic camouflage, but the overall effect of the floor may be reminiscent of a hotel lobby or airport waiting area.

Another disadvantage, for some households, is that carpet tends to harbor house mites, which can trigger allergic reactions and asthma. Cat and dog fleas are also rather fond of it, and a serious infestation can be difficult to eradicate. Synthetic fibers, such as polypropylene, have been identified by environmental lobbyists as posing a degree of health risk, while nylon can cause a buildup of static electricity.

Types and characteristics

Before choosing a carpet, familiarize yourself with the options available. You need to consider the fiber content, texture, construction, pile weight, and density—not to mention color and pattern. Don't be tempted to base your decision on appearance alone. A good underlay is also essential and will add years to the life of the carpet.

Grade and pile weight

Different grades of carpet are suitable for different locations. Some can take only light wear, as in bedrooms, while others will stand up to the heavy traffic of halls and stairs.

The resilience of a carpet is a function of its density, in other words, how closely the fibers are packed together, and has little to do with the actual thickness or depth of the pile. To assess density, press the pile down with your thumb to see how quickly it springs back into shape; if it recovers almost immediately, it is dense and will wear well. You can also gauge the density of woven carpets by examining the back to see if the tufts are tightly spaced or by digging your fingers down into the pile to the base, then spreading the tufts apart to see if there is much room between them.

Right and below: The wild irreverence of leopardskin carpet is a stylish and playful addition to a clean-lined home. Covering the base of the bed gives a sense of comfort. Down the stairs, the pattern is eye-catching.

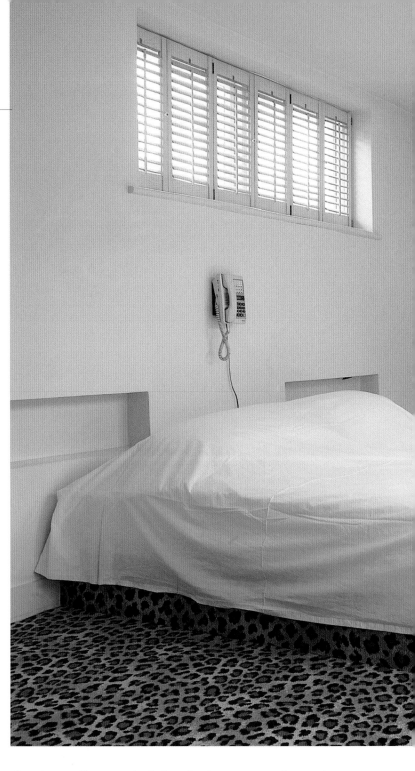

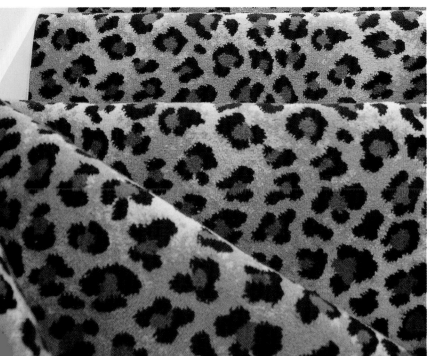

There is no uniform standard of grading in carpet manufacture, but pile weights are usually given on the label and provide a useful benchmark:

Light domestic use, for example, bedrooms, though not necessarily young children's bedrooms, and other areas that are not heavily used: up to 28 ounces per square yard.

Light to medium domestic use, for example, living rooms: 30 ounces per square yard.

Medium to heavy domestic use, for example, family living rooms: 34 ounces per square yard.

Heavy domestic use, for example, on stairs, landings, and in entranceways, especially where there is a direct link with outside: 35 ounces per square metre.

Axminster carpet is made by inserting the pile into the backing from above, then cutting it, a method that allows a large number of colors to be used, since strands do not have to run along the back. (The term is confusing, since it does not refer to the products of the Axminster carpet factory, which was originally established in England in the middle of the 18th century to make hand-knotted pile carpets.) Axminster carpets are cut pile and often highly (sometimes luridly) patterned. They are usually expensive and hard wearing, and are often chosen for commercial locations.

Wilton carpet is named after the factory established in southwestern England around 1740. The pile yarn is continuously woven into the weft, leaving loops, which can be left uncut, cut to make smooth-cut pile, or sculpted in a mix of cut and uncut loops for relief patterns. The method of manufacture means that fewer colors can be used, normally only up to five (unlike the Axminster construction), since the different colors must be carried through the backing until required by the pattern. Wilton is more usually synonymous, however, with plain smooth-cut pile carpet of high quality and corresponding expense.

Flat-weave carpets, as the name implies, have no pile at all. They are normally made of wool, or have a very high percentage of wool, and have become increasingly popular in recent years. Pale, muted, or natural colors are typical, as well as stripes or plaid patterns that run through the weave. The effect is tailored and discreetly elegant, with a similar aesthetic to the finer natural-fiber coverings such as jute or sisal.

Tufted carpets These are the product of high-speed modern manufacturing techniques developed during the 1950s. The pile is inserted into the prewoven base material by needles and may be left uncut in loops, sliced for cut pile, or produced in a combination of the two. The backing is coated with adhesive to keep the pile in place, and a second backing may be added for increased strength, sometimes incorporating a foam-rubber underlay. Tufted carpets tend to be cheaper than woven varieties. Solid colors are standard, but flecked and simple printed patterns are also available.

Nonwoven carpets At the cheapest end of the market are nonwoven carpets, which are made by bonding pile fibers (usually synthetic) to the backing with adhesive, flocking the fibers electrostatically to the backing, or needle-punching them into the backing and sticking with adhesive. Some nonwoven types are designed to resemble woven cord. These carpets are generally thin and lack resilience, making them uncomfortable to walk on; commercial versions are very hard-wearing. They have no pile. Many carpet tiles are made this way.

Carpet construction

The main types of carpet construction are woven, tufted, and nonwoven, although the method of construction is not necessarily an indication of quality. Nonwoven types are generally cheap and often look it, but there may be little qualitative difference between well-constructed woven and tufted carpets of similar pile weight. There are also flat-weave carpets, with no pile at all. Carpet is available in different widths—anything over 6 feet wide is designated "broadloom".

Woven carpets These have the pile woven along with the backing, which makes them strong, hard wearing, and generally fairly expensive. There are several styles:

Carpet pile and textural variation

Carpet texture is not solely affected by the fibers used—the pile makes an important contribution. Effects range from smooth, plush, velvety surfaces to self-colored patterns in tight low loops. Some of the more common ones are:

Cut pile, in which the pile loops are cut to make tufts of yarn that stand upright, is smooth and matte. Because of its smoothness, it may show footmarks or shading.

Velvet or **velour pile** is a very smooth and soft version of cut pile. It is quite durable and easy to clean, but again may show footmarks or shading.

Loop pile has uncut loops; the longer the loops, the bulkier and lighter the carpet. Patterns can be created by loops at different

Right and below, far right: Customized carpet, one made to the individual's own specification, allows exciting and original effects to be created. In this sleek modern interior, for instance, a pathway of subtly contrasting color has been created, which deliberately leads the eye through the space.

Right: Texture is an important dimension to consider when choosing a carpet. This shaggy pile carpet in metallic gray contrasts with the clean lines of the furniture.

levels. Top of the line is Brussels weave, an expensive, hard-wearing form of loop pile in which the warp and weft yarns are equal in number. Cord is a tight low loop pile that resembles corduroy and is very durable. Berber is a loop pile made of natural undyed wool, although the term also applies to variegated or flecked wool. It makes a good all-purpose carpet.

Cut-and-loop pile, as its name implies, mixes cut-and-loop pile types to create relief patterns. It is normally available in solid colors only. Patterns, including herringbone, diamonds, and basketweave, are made by cutting some loops and leaving others uncut at the same level or at higher or lower levels.

Hard twist (or **frisé cut pile**) is a type of cut pile in which the fibers are twisted and set to give a tighter texture that does not fluff—nor does it show footmarks or shading. It wears well and is ideal for stairs and areas of heavy traffic.

Shag pile refers to carpets with a pile up to 2 inches long. Suitable only for light use, it should not be used on the stairs, where it may be hazardous. Shag pile is hard to keep clean and mats and tangles easily. The deep pile can provide an attractive home for cat and dog fleas.

Carpet composition

Many different fibers, both synthetic and natural, singly as well as blended, are currently used to make carpets. The fiber content is one of the most important factors determining the price, appearance, and performance of a carpet.

The finest carpets have always been, and still are, allwool. Yet the difference between natural and synthetic materials is not as great as it once was, and the majority of carpets sold today are blends, with the synthetic component lending strength as well as bringing down the price to more reasonable levels. The most common fibers used in carpet manufacture are:

Wool The classic carpet fiber. Nothing feels or looks as good. Warm, soft, and springy underfoot, it does not dent or flatten easily and is fairly straightforward to clean, as well as being antistatic and flameresistant. The best choice for the environmentally conscious, wool is a natural material and an expensive one. Some of the finest carpet wool comes from New Zealand. A pure wool carpet is not particularly durable, however. An 80% wool, 20% nylon or 40% wool and 60% acrylic produces a more hard-wearing all-purpose blend. Pure or blended wool carpets will require moth protection treatment.

Linen shares the natural credentials of wool but has more limited applications in carpet terms. Linen is extremely expensive and far from long lasting as a floor covering, but it is elegant and unconventional. To maximize its performance, linen is best laid over a thick underlay.

Acrylic is a synthetic fiber that bears a close resemblance to wool. It is, however, much more likely to be flattened by heavy furniture and to show dirt; it also has poor flame resistance. An acrylic carpet is cheaper than wool but generally more expensive than a nylon one.

Nylon is a very strong and durable synthetic fiber often used in blends with wool. In spite of its generally poor image, good-quality nylon is very soft and available in a wide choice of colors. It can be expensive. Some nylon carpet is treated to make it less static, and stain-resistant types are also available. Cheap versions, though, have rather a harsh texture and soil easily. All nylon melts rather than burns.

Polyester is a cheap synthetic fiber that is soft, durable and easy to clean. It is not as springy as acrylic and is often used to make shag- pile carpet. It has poor flame resistance.

Polypropylene is another cheap synthetic fiber now being increasingly used in good-quality blends because it is very hard wearing and stain resistant. It flattens easily, though, so is not suitable for deep-pile carpets. It is also flammable and does not take dye well.

Viscose is another cheap synthetic frequently used in poor-quality carpeting. It never looks other than cheap. It is also flammable and easily soiled.

Custom carpeting

Carpet is available in a vast variety of colors, textures, and patterns. Nevertheless, there is still a market for custom design—made-to-order services exist to create unique carpets to individual specifications. If you want to commission a new carpet from a historical fragment or document or devise an original pattern incorporating a specific motif, custom design is the answer. There are textile designers specializing in custom carpeting who can also interpret a style for you. Such services are expensive.

Carpet tiles

At the opposite end of the market from custom designs, carpet tiles combine the appearance of carpeting with a practical format. They have a much wider application in commercial interiors than in the home, and their aesthetic tends to reflect this. Carpet tiles come in a choice of different-size squares, fibers, construction, and backings, and in plain and patterned designs. They can be laid to resemble an unbroken expanse of carpet or in various tile patterns combining different colors or designs.

The advantage of carpet tiles is that they can be easily and quickly laid and just as easily moved or replaced, making it possible to deal with patches of wear individually rather than go to the expense and trouble of re-covering an entire floor. They also allow easy access to underfloor services. In the home, they are perhaps most useful in areas likely to receive a great deal of wear and tear but where a soft surface is still desirable, such as in children's rooms.

Carpet tiles vary in quality and hence appearance: the better commercial versions can be quite handsome, but cheaper nonwoven, mass-market tiles are often fairly dreary. They can be stuck down or laid loose. Moving the tiles around from time to time will distribute wear evenly and is often a better idea than replacing a few worn tiles with conspicuously new ones.

Underlay

A good-quality underlay will prolong the life of your carpet and make the floor warmer, quieter, and more comfortable to walk on. Underlay compensates for any slight unevenness in the subfloor and provides a barrier against dirt and moisture. Quality is determined more by the material than its thickness; very thick

Above top: Flat-weave carpet in a striking black-and-white plaid adds great character to a tartan room.

Above: The same plaid carpet is dramatically offset by oxblood walls on the stairway.

Opposite page, far left: A classic pattern makes a suitable foil for a period room.

Left: White cord carpet, matched with deep white baseboards and bed base, creates a great sense of light and expansiveness.

underlay is best avoided, since it can make the floor too soft and giving. All fabric-backed carpet requires underlay; foam-backed carpet should be laid on felt paper to prevent the foam backing from sticking to the floor.

Felt underlays are best used with quality woven carpets. These natural underlays consist of jute, wool or other animal hair, or a mixture of both. Foam or rubber underlays tend to be used under tufted rather than woven carpet. The best have a firm texture that does not crumble. These underlays should not be used on stairs, over underfloor heating, or in damp conditions. There are also underlays that are a mixture of felt and rubber.

Choosing and buying carpet

Visit a carpet supplier or the flooring department of a good department store to compare different types and ask for samples to take home and live with for a while before committing yourself to a decision. Large retailers with big turnovers offer competitive prices; suppliers of brand-name carpeting tend to be more expensive. For bargains, try alternative sources specializing in room-size remnants or ends of rolls—the choice will be more limited, but the savings may be considerable. Many of these outlets sell carpet originally designed for heavy-duty commercial use, which means that larger remnants are often available.

To make accurate price comparisons you need to take accurate measurements of the area you intend to carpet (see page 167). Many suppliers provide a measuring service; all should be able to advise how best to minimize wastage and reduce the need for seams. Remember to include the cost of underlay, grippers, and other accessories, as well as the cost of fitting.

Laying

Carpet should be laid on a dry, even subfloor that has been properly prepared. Baseboards can stay in place, but doors may need to be removed and planed to accommodate the increased height of the final floor. A well-laid carpet will last much longer than one that has been inexpertly installed. It is possible to install foam-backed carpet yourself (see pages 178–79), provided you are strong enough to manipulate the rolls, but laying fabric-backed carpet demands skill and proper tools.

Maintenance

Everyone knows that keeping carpet in good condition means frequent vacuuming. Dirt is not merely unsightly and unhygienic, it works its way down into the pile, where it wears away at the fibers. Brushing or sweeping may tackle surface debris, but only a vacuum cleaner can reach the base of the pile. Avoid undue indentation by placing furniture cups under the legs of sofas, chairs, and heavy tables. See pages 180–81 for stain-prevention techniques.

Natural-fiber coverings

Flooring made from natural fibers, including sisal, coir, seagrass, and rush, has won many hearts in recent years, making the transition from the eccentric to the mainstream with remarkable speed. And yet, although such materials convey a fresh, contemporary image, they have one of the most ancient pedigrees of all types of flooring — a history of use that dates back centuries.

Long before medieval owners covered the drafty stone floors of their castles and manor houses with a layer of disposable rush and straw, the ancient Egyptians were weaving mats from bulrushes. Until a couple of decades ago, however, most people were acquainted with these materials only as the ubiquitous coir doormat or the serviceable utility covering on the floors of old houses. All that was before modern production techniques transformed natural-fiber flooring into a serious alternative to carpet, available in widths that could be installed wall to wall.

The renewed popularity of these products owes much to the modern desire to live with natural materials. Unlike the majority of carpet on the market, which contain at least some percentage of synthetic ingredients, natural-fiber coverings are wholly natural, from sustainable resources, and affordable. They look authentic, too, with their natural neutral tones and nubbly woven textures, offering a pared-down simplicity that is also in tune with contemporary taste. Not that colors are limited to the muted beige shades of the basic ingredients; strong, rich shades and graphic patterns have been introduced to widen the decorative potential. Aesthetically speaking, these coverings are very versatile, easily

Right: Seagrass is the smoothest of the natural fibers. It is also naturally stain resistant, and therefore practically impossible to dye. The biscuit tones of the basic ingredient are, however, inherently pleasing, and the nubbliness of the weave gives it a dimensional character. Here, matting laid loose over stripped floorboards heightens the elegance of period decorations and furnishings.

Opposite, top: Jute is the least tough of the natural fibers and cannot withstand a high degree of wear. But its softness gives it a special degree of refinement, ideal for locations that do not see the heavy traffic of daily household use. The muted stripe of this jute weave is emphasized by laying the pattern in the direction of the natural light source.

Opposite, below: Coarser and more overtly textural, sisal is one of the most popular of the natural fibers. Here it serves as a base for a contemporary seating area.

Below, left to right: Jute (bleached); jute (unbleached); seagrass; coir (bouclé); coir (herringbone); seagrass (herringbone); sisal (bouclé); sisal (bouclé); and sisal.

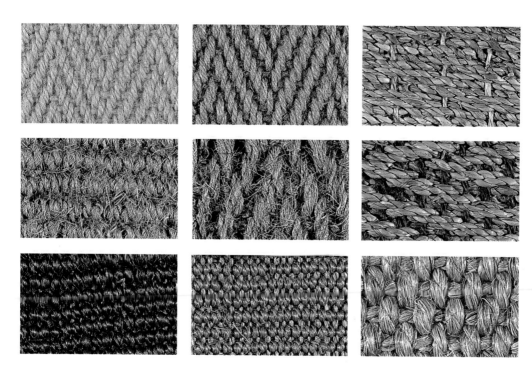

accommodating every decorative look — town or country, period or contemporary. Ecologically sound, full of character, and infinitely adaptable, natural-fiber coverings deserve their status as classics in the making.

Most natural fibers wear reasonably well, although jute is the least durable and will not stand up to heavy traffic. It is also considerably softer than the other natural fibers, for which reason it is the only one that approaches the comfort of carpet. The prickliness of coir and (to a lesser extent) sisal can be rather unpopular: children in particular find them rather inhospitable.

Natural-fiber coverings are not as resilient underfoot as carpet, although using an underlay improves the resilience. With the exception of rush, they are impractical for damp or humid areas such as bathrooms or conservatories, and also busy kitchens and utility rooms. Seagrass can be slippery, and really coarse weaves of coir and rush are hazardous on stairs because heels can easily catch. By and large, most natural fibers shrug off dirt and debris, but they do stain. Protective treatment is advisable. All of these types of flooring are antistatic. Most are backed with latex, which prevents the accumulation of grit or dirt underneath, and makes installation simple; all can be laid wall to wall. Most types compare favorably in price with carpeting and, like carpeting, require professional fitting.

Opposite: Many natural materials are now used to make floor coverings. Their strength and visual interest derives from the weaves. Here banana-fiber matting has a look of elegant restraint in a light-filled dining area.

Left: Raffia matting accentuates the British colonial style of this airy living area, with its wicker furniture and pleasing neutral colours.

Top: While there is a strong resemblance among the natural-fiber materials, there are variations in practical performance. Seagrass is very durable and stain resistant.

Above left: Rush makes a good foil for bright rugs or an elegant and stylish floor in its own right.

Above right: Seagrass, like most natural-fiber coverings, can be laid wall to wall.

Types and characteristics

Each type of natural fiber has distinctive attributes, in both practical and aesthetic terms. With the exception of rush, these floorings come with latex backing, but the materials are also available in the form of mats, runners, and rugs.

Seagrass is the smoothest of the natural fibers, which makes it more comfortable underfoot. The name refers to the fact that the crop is grown like rice in paddy fields that are flooded with seawater during the growing season. Seagrass is tough, cheap, and antistatic. Because the hard fiber is virtually impermeable, it does not stain like other natural fibers and shrugs off dirt. This characteristic, however, also means that seagrass cannot be dyed. Nevertheless, the basic natural color can be enhanced by incorporating colored weft strings in black, green, red, or blue.

Seagrass can be used almost anywhere in the home and can make a successful floor covering in kitchens, bathrooms, and sunrooms provided it is not subject to excessive moisture or spills. It should be laid on stairs only with the grain parallel to the tread; otherwise, its smooth surface would be too slippery.

Coir is a fiber that comes from the coconut husk, from which it is beaten after the husk is soaked in fresh water. It is traditionally used for making doormats and sacks; being naturally coarse and prickly, it is not especially comfortable for bedrooms or children's

Far left: Sisal matting domesticates hard flooring in a hot climate.

Center left: Coir introduces a natural element on a high-level walkway.

Above left and below: Seagrass and coir can be used very effectively and practically on stairs, provided the coarser weaves are avoided.

Above: Seagrass enhances the Oriental mood of this burnished decor.

rooms. Very coarse, loose coir weaves are not suitable for stairs; heels will catch. Standard coir has an innately rustic look, but there are more sophisticated designs, with striped or chevron patterns in rich reds, blues, and greens. Coir comes in a variety of weaves, including bouclé, basketweave, diamond, and herringbone, and, blended with sisal, it now comes in tile format. The standard version is cheap and durable, but it does stain.

Sisal is an exceptionally versatile fiber in terms of its decorative potential and performance, and is, accordingly, the most popular of the natural fibers. The basic fiber comes from the leaves of *Agave sisalana*, a dark-green spiky bush that grows in the subtropics and has a traditional use in making rope and twine.

The texture of sisal is between the hairiness of coir and the softness of jute, which makes it durable enough to take heavy traffic but still acceptable for bare feet. It is easy to dye and comes in a variety of shades, patterns, and weaves, as well as in wool blends. Inevitably, its readiness to accept dye means a corresponding lack of stain resistance. Stain-inhibiting treatments are advisable. Sisal is more expensive than coir or seagrass.

Right: Sisal, laid wall to wall as an integral covering, sets the tone for neutral decor based around natural themes, which is easy on the eyes.

Above far right: A blond-on-blond effect has been achieved here by insetting coarse sisal within an expanse of gleaming hardwood parquet.

Below far right: Edge-bound sisal matting is loose-laid over sisal flooring for a layering of texture that adds visual interest.

Above left and right: An original and economical treatment for a large contemporary space combines sisal matting inset within an expanse of board sheeting. Tonally very similar, the effect of the two flooring surfaces is a subtle change of texture underfoot with no compromise of the spacious quality.

Left: Sisal is easy to dye, which means that it is available in a wide choice of soft natural colors and patterns. Designs include striped runners and bold chevrons, as well as more pictorial effects, such as this "needlepoint" sisal mat.

Jute comes from a plant native to subtropical regions of India and has been exported to the West since the 18th century for use in rope making and as carpet backing. The fiber is stripped by hand from the stalks of the plant, which have been softened in water. Jute is slightly cheaper than the best sisal but far less durable. It is soft enough to be more than welcome in the bedroom but will not stand up to heavy wear and requires stain protection. It is available in a choice of elegant weaves and in natural and bleached tones, as well as pastel and rich colors.

Rush or medieval matting makes a heavy, robust flooring that can be used in a wide range of locations. It is inherently countrified in appearance, yet it can also make a stylish contemporary floor. The matting is made of hand-braided strips of rush, each 3½ inches wide, which are sewn together to make a room-size covering (which is laid loose) or mats of any dimension. Medieval matting is at the top end of the natural-fiber price range. It should not be used on stairs because it is too smooth and slippery. Rush matting needs regular sprinkling with water to maintain its condition and makes a good flooring for naturally damp areas such as sunrooms and bathrooms, provided there is adequate ventilation.

Laying

Like carpet, natural fiber coverings require a dry, level, even sub-floor that has been properly prepared. An underlay is not essential, but it will serve to correct any slight imperfections in the subfloor and provide extra resilience and wear resistance. However, if you intend to use these materials on stairs, an underlay is always a good idea as it will make the covering much more durable.

Before installation, natural-fiber coverings should be laid out in the area where they are to be installed for 48 hours in order to acclimatize the fibers to the ambient humidity levels. Latex-backed

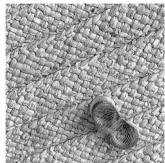

Above: Rush matting tends to be rather more expensive than other types of natural fiber coverings and needs regular sprinkling with water.

Right: Absence of strong color need not mean absence of vitality, provided textures are contrasted for depth of character.

Far left: The simplicity of rush matting and pale walls is contrasted by the bold use of color on the woodwork to create a calm, timeless hallway.

Center left: Braided rush matting goes well with country-house style decorations.

natural-fiber coverings should be stuck down all over, either directly to the subfloor or to the underlay that has been stapled to the floor. Laying requires the skilss of a professional. The recommended adhesive leaves no sticky residue, which means the covering can be taken up at a later date without damage to the subfloor. Seams can be tightly butted up or taped. Gripper rods around the perimeter of the room in addition to the adhesive also help to prevent subsequent shrinkage.

Maintenance

Many natural-fiber coverings are susceptible to wear from castors, so it is best to have additional protection under chair and sofa legs. Spiked heels are also best avoided. Bright sunshine may cause fading in some varieties. Natural floor coverings react differently and usually (with the exception of medieval matting) adversely to humidity. Coir expands with moisture and may wrinkle and buckle. As it dries out, joints may open up. Sisal, on the other hand, shrinks when wet. In very damp conditions, all natural fibers will rot.

For regular maintenance, all of these floorings should be vacuumed. Never wash or shampoo. Coir, sisal, and jute are best treated with a stain-inhibitor. Tackle spills immediately, blotting up as much as possible from the surface before staining has a chance to occur. Let muddy tracks dry out and then brush along the grain and vacuum.

Rugs

Superficially, rugs are finishing touches, the decorative flourishes that make rooms look well dressed. However, both practically and aesthetically rugs can be a key element in making a room complete, rather than merely optional accessories.

Rugs domesticate floors. They provide an essential layer of comfort, warmth, and sound protection that helps to mitigate some of the disadvantages of hard flooring, such as stone, hard tiles, and wood. Rugs allow you to have your cake and eat it, too, offering a soft surface to meet bare feet by the bedside or a cozy place to curl up in front of the fire without the need to carpet throughout the entire space. Unlike other types of flooring, rugs do not commit you to a permanent arrangement. They can be moved from home to home or room to room; brought out in winter and rolled away in summer.

Rugs are no less defining elements visually. A rug transforms a sofa and chairs into a seating circle; a series of rugs in an open-plan space gives what could be just so much empty floor area a sense of enclosure and proportion. Rugs bring depth and character to

Below: Rugs that display the soft colors of vegetable dyes can be layered for a sympathetic blend of pattern.

decorative schemes, adding vitality to neutral backgrounds and providing a coordinating element where rooms are more richly colored or patterned. A beautiful rug can serve as a room's signature, the foundation for the entire decorative approach, as well as provide pleasure in its own right.

Rugs or carpets were once the treasured possessions of the privileged few. Until the 18th century, fine carpets were never laid on the floor, but draped over tables or hung on walls. Today, there

Above: Contemporary rugs make floor-level art. Bold geometric or abstract designs have great vitality.

are many rugs that still merit this degree of reverence, glorious antique collector's items costing a king's ransom. But the majority of rugs now available, even Oriental or Persian ones, are within the reach of the average household, and many flat-weave rugs are positively cheap.

For centuries, carpets were synonymous with rugs of Oriental or Middle Eastern provenance, normally fine knotted examples with a pile surface. Knotted carpets have been produced in various regions of the world since antiquity, but they only began to appear in the West in large quantities after the establishment of reliable trading routes during the 16th and 17th centuries. By the

Above: A new departure in soft flooring, rugs made of paper twine have a crisp, graphic look, ideal for contemporary settings.

18th century, the first factories producing a similar type of knotted carpet were established in Europe, and the spread of influence then became went both ways—Middle Eastern and Oriental carpets designs began to reflect European taste. This cross-fertilization of ideas between East and West is no less marked today, with modern designers seeking inspiration and buyers from large retail chains in Europe and North America commissioning carpets, dhurries, and kilims direct from local manufacturers in designs and colors most likely to appeal to their Western customers. The results are often pleasing abstractions of ethnic patterns and motifs that lack the more overtly tribal appearance of traditional designs.

The past few decades have seen an explosion of interest in more humble ethnic weaves, such as kilims and dhurries, flat weaves with naive geometric patterns. These eminently affordable rugs have a contemporary quality and freshness that works well in modern interiors. At the same time, the current crafts revival has brought the work of modern rug designers and makers to the fore, and a wide range of original rugs can be found, as one-of-a-kind commissions, in limited runs, or in mass-market quantities. All in all, there is more scope for floor-level art than ever before. Prices vary enormously. Simple cotton rag rugs cost no more than an average restaurant meal, while a good quality Persian might set you back as much as a couture evening dress—and more. Rather than compromise on quality, it is often better to opt for a different type of rug altogether: what would not buy you a very exciting Oriental might buy you a superb kilim, for example.

Types and characteristics

Rugs and carpets vary in construction and material as well as in provenance, color, pattern, and design. The terminology can be confusing: "Oriental," for instance may be loosely applied to any carpet from the Near, Middle, or Far East. At the upper end of the market, rugs are a subject for the connoisseur, with variations of design classified according to region or tribe as well as period. At the other end are the simple homespun styles made from scraps of cotton or wool, originally out of necessity, of course, using whatever was on hand.

Knotted carpets, with a pile surface, include various kinds of Turkish, Persian, and Chinese rugs. The quality of the carpet is a function of its density, with the finest having as many as 1,000 knots per square inch. Most of these carpets are made of wool, but very luxurious versions are made in silk.

Chinese carpets are thick knotted carpets made from wool or silk, often in light, clear colors, typically blue, yellow, peach, and white. The motifs are fairly widely spaced and often feature stylized flowers, birds, butterflies, dragons, or figures; and the surface of the pile is sometimes cut for a sculpted relief effect. This type of "Oriental" rug is now made not only in China—Iran and India produce fine examples—and the best are expensive.

Tibetan carpets come from the remote regions of Tibet and Nepal. They are hand knotted in wool, and can be of very high quality and corresponding expense. Traditional designs and colors may show a classic Chinese influence, although rugs commissioned by Western buyers display a blend of classic and contemporary motifs.

Turkish carpets is a term loosely employed to refer to a range of different types of carpet, hand- or machine made, from the Near and Middle East, with much of the production centering on the Anatolian region of Turkey. They are distinguished from Persian carpets by the type of knot used for the pile, known as the Ghiordes knot, which is tied symmetrically on two adjacent warp threads. Typically, designs are stylized nature motifs, sometimes with central medallions; there are also prayer rugs, featuring an arch whose apex is to be pointed in the direction of Mecca. Wool is sometimes mixed with coarser goat hair. During the latter part of the 19th century, the use of chemical or aniline dyes resulted in

harsh coloring, but modern Turkish rug producers are now returning to the use of traditional vegetable dyes. Some weaving cooperatives are collaborating with Western designers and suppliers to produce modern designs with an ethnic flavor.

Persian carpets represent the height of weaving artistry. Technically, they are distinguished by the use of the Persian knot, in which yarn is twisted around one warp thread and under the adjacent thread, allowing the construction of a very dense pile; each rug represents hours and hours of intensive work. Made of wool or silk, patterns are rich and detailed, with stylized or naturalistic flowers, leaves, animals, and birds scattered over the ground. Some designs recall a garden of paradise; others feature the tree of life, prayer arches, and central medallions. The *gul*, a stylized flower motif in the form of a rounded octagon also known as an "elephant's foot," and the *boteh*, a stylized leaf (similar to the motif in a paisley pattern), are also typical. The finest Persian carpets ever made date from between the 16th and 18th centuries and are now museum pieces; quality control has helped to keep modern standards high. True Persian carpets are made in Iran and other parts of central Asia, and are often classified by specific town or region of origin, such as Isfahan and Tabriz. The best are handknotted, but there are also machine-made versions from small factories, as well as reproductions made in Pakistan, Bulgaria, and the West (sometimes unscrupulously passed off as originals). Background colors are often deep red or blue. Good-quality Persian carpets improve with age and should last for generations.

Turkoman or Bokhara carpets are wool rugs sourced from a wide area across central Asia, including Pakistan, Afghanistan, and Turkmenistan. Many of these rugs feature the characteristic *gul* motif. Colors are typically dark, rusty red, black, and blue. Bokhara, an important trading center in central Asia, has become the general term for carpets woven by nomadic peoples of the region.

Caucasian carpets include a variety of different types of carpet, from knotted pile to flat weaves, which derive from the Caucasus region between the Black Sea and the Caspian Sea. Motifs are stylized and often naive, with a graphic use of bright color and intricate borders. Some designs are similar to very simplified Persian patterns; *soumak* are flat-weave carpets with threads left loose at the back.

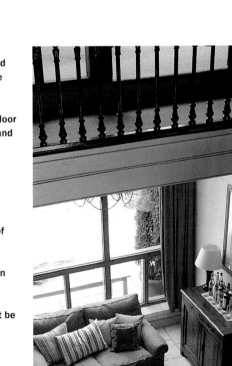

Opposite, above: Good-quality carpets are knotted by hand and colored using natural vegetable dyes.

Opposite, below: Natural-fiber floor coverings make an ideal base and an excellent foil for brightly colored rugs.

Center left: The rich, luminous reds of these Oriental carpets introduce visual warmth and complement the earthy tones of the exposed brickwork. Rugs provide a perfect means of defining distinct areas within an open-plan space.

Left: Rugs on bare boards must be laid over nonslip matting.

Right: Kilims, with their bold graphic patterns and strong contrasting colors, provide vivid focal points. Here, the decorating scheme has drawn its inspiration from the colors displayed in the rug itself, to create a rich yet unifying effect.

Kilim is the generic Persian term for a coarse woolen flat-weave rug and is used today to refer to carpets hand woven by nomadic peoples in the Middle East (specifically Afghanistan and Turkey) and North Africa. Colors vary, but rich reds, golds, creams, blacks, and blues are typical; designs vary, too, but are generally geometric and bold. Kilims are available in a wide range of sizes, including runners, and in different qualities. Good antique kilims are the most expensive, although they are still reasonably priced compared to the finer Persian carpets. Kilims are not as durable as knotted pile carpets.

Dhurrie is the Indian version of the kilim, a flat-weave rug usually made of cotton. Colors are often much less intense—almost somber, compared to kilims—with the pale tones of gray, pink, ocher, and light blue being typical. Although dhurries have been

Above: Flat-weave carpets, such as kilims and dhurries, are at the more affordable end of the price spectrum. The pale tones of this traditional rug suit the simple modern setting.

Left and far left: Vegetable dyes produce rich, glorious color without stridency.

Opposite above: Rugs layered on the floor complement ethnic-style furnishings for a flavor of the *souk* or bazaar.

Opposite below: Naive motifs are part of the charm of handmade rugs. Antique originals are highly prized.

Opposite far right: A dhurrie in cool blues tones happily with Swedish-style decor.

woven since antiquity, it is only in relatively recent times that these rugs have become widely popular in the West. There has been an exchange of color ideas and designs between Western retailers and Indian producers: simple stripes, checks, zigzags, and chevrons predominate. Dhurries do not provide much in the way of warmth or sound insulation, but their crisp, clean designs are much in tune with modern taste. They are affordable, and reversible, and some can be machine washed, although shrinkage is likely.

Aubusson carpets are tapestry-woven smooth-faced rugs, which take their name from the products of the original Aubusson factory established in France in the 18th century. Designs are typically feminine and floral, in light, pretty colors.

Needlepoint rugs, traditionally worked in tent stitch on a canvas backing, have the appearance of tapestry, with widely spaced floral motifs on a plain pale or dark ground. Hand-worked needlepoint rugs were common in early American homes, the product of hours of painstaking toil; machine-made reproductions are now available.

Serape is the name for a thin flat-weave rug or blanket from Mexico and the southwestern United States, woven in searingly bright colors and often in striped patterns.

Shag-pile rugs include the wooly Greek *flokati*, normally white or off-white, and the Finnish *rya*, a long-pile rug in strong contemporary designs and bright colors.

Felt rugs include the *numdah* from Kashmir, which is a cheap, soft nonwoven carpet often featuring naive motifs embroidered on a pale background. Nursery versions with simple animals and alphabets are popular. Numdahs wear out quickly, show dirt very readily, and don't clean easily.

Rag, hooked, and braided rugs are examples of simple folk weaves that were originally made—out of necessity—from scraps of cotton material or old clothing, roughly stitched or looped together, hooked through a canvas backing, or braided and sewn. Rag, hooked, and braided rugs define a certain kind of countrified style

that is Scandinavian and North European in origin, but also strongly associated with the homespun look of colonial American interiors. These rugs are not difficult to make, albeit time-consuming, but mass-market versions are widely available and extremely cheap. Antique originals, on the other hand, are collector's items.

Slightly more sophisticated are flat weaves in cotton or wool, often in soft natural colors and subtle textured patterns. Classic designs include striped runners, a feature of traditional Scandinavian interiors, where they were often laid around the perimeter of the room to make a carpeted walkway over bare boards. Some of the colors used in modern interpretations are also inspired by their Scandinavian origins. Runners are also highly suitable for hallways and stairs, as they can be turned periodically to distribute wear evenly.

Right: Beautiful blues make a serene combination in complementary patterns. The striped design of the flat-weave rug, checked pillow covers, and webbed seat provide a change where color is restricted to one part of the spectrum.

Below: A banded carpet in flat woven wool takes center stage.

Opposite top: A woven cotton rug laid over fine jute is the essence of pure style.

Opposite bottom (left and right): Flat-weave cotton rugs make versatile – and washable – coverings for all areas of the home.

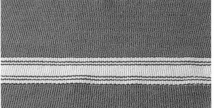

Choosing and buying rugs

For modern rugs, craft organizations promoting the work of new designers and craftspeople can be a useful starting point if you are looking for a one-of-a-kind original. Otherwise, retailers and department stores increasingly stock a wide range of rugs of all kinds, both traditional and contemporary, and the volume of sales generally guarantees sensible pricing. The selection of stock generally includes area rugs (essentially unfitted or loose-laid carpet) and machine-made reproductions of traditional Persian, Oriental, or Turkish carpets as well as the genuine articles. Some specialist suppliers produce reissues of classic patterns by famous designers such as William Morris or early modernists such as Eileen Gray. Natural fiber floorings are also available in the form of runners, rugs, or room-size mats from the same type of outlets that supply wall-to-wall natural flooring.

In many areas of the world, the carpet dealer has long been viewed as a trickster or con artist. Buying Oriental rugs, antique or new, hand knotted or machine made, still demands a degree of expertise and wariness on the part of the purchaser. There is no real substitute for a working familiarity with different types and qualities of rug. If you intend to make a serious investment, it is best to study the subject in some detail and then take a long hard look at what is available from different sources before making a final choice. Real quality is normally more or less self-evident. A fine rug has a certain luminous look. The design will be crisp and clear, rather than blurred; the colors rich, not muddy. Rugs produced in areas of the world where the light is strong are often quite bright to

Below: Relief textures introduce a new dynamic to restrained neutral shades. The effect is similar to other, more traditional, self- **colored patterns such as damask, but with a fresh, contemporary edge that lends wit and flair to a modern interior.**

Left and above: A beautiful rug, whether contemporary or traditional, can provide the signature of a room's decoration and style. Here the soft colors of the rug are picked up in the upholstery and furniture in slightly stronger tones, while the loose abstract design creates a counterpoint to the strong modern lines. The pale hardwood flooring makes a discreet background surface.

Below: Contemporary art rugs can be commissioned directly from designers and craftspeople, or acquired through a craft gallery or similar outlet. A less expensive proposition are the modern rugs available from retailers that share a similar aesthetic. This careful composition in blocks and bands introduces discreet color to a basic neutral decor.

Above, far left (and detail): The ultimate custom flooring —a shaped rug inset with studded copper panels brings a touch of fantasy and glamour to a hallway soberly paneled in wood.

Below, far left: Definitely not for the retiring, a rich red rug patterned with squiggles of electric color adds a jazzy touch to postmodern decor.

Left: Bold bands of rainbow colors make a striking entrance. Brilliant color is positive and refreshing in hallways and provides a welcoming first impression.

Below: A dramatic modern rug makes a sweeping semicircular pathway around a bed. The inset panel is slate: a quirky use for an old bath panel.

Western eyes, but the colors will mature and soften with time. Rugs made of wool that has been vegetable dyed age gracefully, the colors fading gently in synchronicity with each other, in contrast to chemically dyed products, which retain a certain harshness.

Good sources include established and reputable dealers who have a long track record in the business, major retail outlets, and, if you know what you are looking for, auctions. At all costs avoid the so-called bankruptcy sales or special "closing down" offers. Buying a rug in its country or region of origin is not a guarantee of either quality or savings: many of the best examples go straight to the export trade, leaving what are often little more than tourist souvenirs in the local markets.

Price is determined by basic quality (such as density, pattern, and material), age, and condition. If you do not mind small signs of wear, such as a bit of fraying or a ragged fringe, you may be able to pick up what is essentially a fine carpet at a bargain price. At the same time, it is important to beware the artificially aged carpet, distressed by bleach or some other means to simulate an antique, but which actually reduces the life. A good dealer will be only too pleased to provide evidence to support a rug's provenance.

Laying

All rugs placed on hard floors should be laid over a nonslip mat to prevent accidents. The extra padding provided by the underlay will also protect the underside of the rug from wear and increase its softness and resilience. Light rugs can be secured by special mesh backing or bonding strips. An underlay pad is also useful if the rug is to be laid over carpet: it will prevent the rug from wrinkling and creeping, and also protect the carpet from staining should the rug prove to be not colorfast.

Practicalitie

s

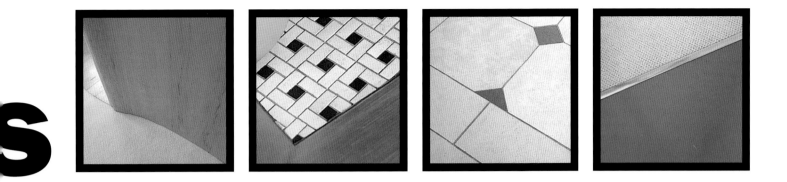

As the preceding chapters have indicated, laying a new floor tends to be a job for the professionals. Unlike other areas of home decoration and improvement, where the skills are relatively simple to acquire and the materials easy to manage, floor laying, with a few exceptions, is considerably more demanding. To begin with, more physical strength is usually required: wood, stone, sheet flooring, carpet rolls, and the larger hard tiles are heavy and unwieldy: some back-breakingly so. Hard materials are often brittle, easy to chip, sheer, crack, or otherwise damage if clumsily handled. They may well be expensive, too, which makes breakages all the more heartrending. A range of special tools may be necessary to cut, fit, and finish the floor, not to mention the special skills that only come with experience. Most floors present at least some obstacles and irregularities—such as pipework, alcoves, or curves—which demand careful planning to circumvent. Floors composed of multiple units, such as tiles, particularly if these are to be laid in patterns, also need to be properly set out for successful results. In most cases, mistakes cannot easily be rectified and a badly laid floor may wear out quickly, be hazardous, or simply be an eyesore.

For all of these reasons, it is best to err on the side of caution and leave it all to the experts. However, if you are reasonably confident of your DIY skills, some types of floor laying are fairly straightforward and instructions for these are included in this section. Even if you do not intend to lay a new floor yourself, there are a number of practical issues that you will need to understand in order to choose the right flooring, buy the right quantity, and commission the work properly.

Know your floor

At the outset, it is important to understand the distinction between floors and flooring. A floor is part of the structure of your home, whereas flooring is the covering applied to the floor. In some cases, floor and flooring may be one and the same thing: wooden floorboards or old flagstones, for example. Most new floors, however, consist of some kind of flooring applied over a structural floor.

There are two main types of floor: solid and suspended. Solid floors occur at ground or basement level and are sometimes known as "direct-to-earth" floors. Most suspended floors are made of wood and consist of two elements: the floor joists, or beams, which span the walls, and floorboards or blockboard sheets laid across the joists. The type of floor structure will determine which floor coverings are suitable. Solid floors and suspended concrete floors can bear more weight than suspended wooden floors. If your chosen flooring is very heavy, you may not be able to use it over a suspended wooden floor at all. If you are in any doubt about the load-bearing capacity of the floor, it is advisable to consult an expert who will be able to do the calculations for you.

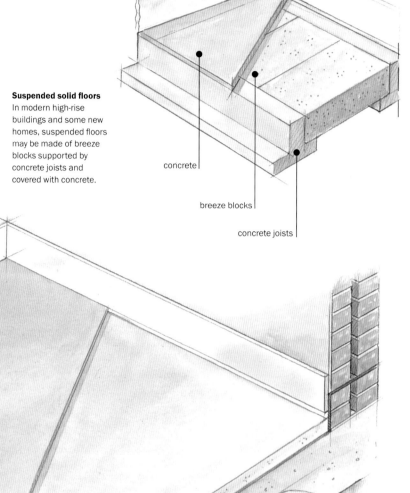

Suspended solid floors
In modern high-rise buildings and some new homes, suspended floors may be made of breeze blocks supported by concrete joists and covered with concrete.

concrete

breeze blocks

concrete joists

gravel

Solid floors
In homes built in the last fifty years, ground floors usually consist of a concrete slab laid over a base of gravel and covered with sand and cement. A dampproof membrane is usually incorporated between the base and the concrete slab to prevent moisture from rising. (Older houses may have flagstones, brick, or hard tiles bedded into the ground; such floors are often not dampproofed.)

concrete slab

sand and cement

floor covering

dampproof or termite barrier

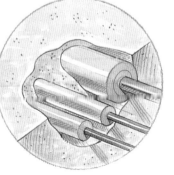

Underfloor services
Pipes and wires can be unseen hazards when new floor coverings are installed. The danger is usually greater in the case of suspended floors; in solid floors, servicing and cables are usually sunk some distance from the surface.

joist   sleeper wall

dampproof membrane in brick

Suspended plank floors
In older row houses, the joists normally run from front to back. At ground level, joists rest in sockets in the external walls and may be partially supported by intermediate "sleeper" walls built up from the ground. Joists at upper levels are often hung from joist hangers attached to the walls and partially supported by partition walls below. At ground or basement levels, joists never rest directly on the ground but are suspended above the level of the dampproof foundations; the sleeper walls on which they rest also have a dampproof course on top.

The effect of humidity
Suspended plank floors tend to move a little with changes in humidity and may need to be covered with masonite or plywood to provide a more rigid, stable, and even base.

Identifying your boards
1 Straight-edged boards will be nailed and therefore can only be joined on a joist. The seams and rows of nails are indications of the position of the under-lying joists. The boards will be laid at right angles to the joists.

2 Tongue-and-groove boards are stable enough to allow for seams between joists. They also give a more seamless finish, without the need for nails through the surface.

Safety precautions
Establish exactly the position of cables and pipework before sawing drilling, or nailing, through floorboards, because pipework and cables are sometimes run in the gap between the joists and boards—which may be quite narrow.

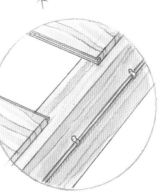

Remedial work

The condition of the subfloor is of critical importance. Before new floor coverings are laid, the subfloor must be inspected for any signs of damage or decay, repaired if necessary, and properly prepared. Failure to treat subfloor deficiencies will result, at best, in a final floor that looks shoddy, and wears badly; at worst, the structural fabric of your home may be weakened. Defects in solid floors, if they are basically sound, dry, and level, can usually be made good by a competent amateur. Any dampness must be eliminated or the floor covering itself will either not stick or, begin to rot. If you don't get to the root cause of the problem, it will only recur.

Wooden subfloors also suffer from damp or insect infestation. If the floor feels bouncy or spongy the joists may be damaged. Wet rot shows up as soft, dark patches on the wood or cracks and splinters. Dry rot may show as musty gray threads or fungal growth. A peppering of fine holes indicates damage by powder-post beetle. In each case professional treatment is imperative. Affected timber must be cut out and the remaining areas sprayed with the appropriate chemical.

Remedying an uneven solid floor

A scratched or pitted surface can be filled by pouring on leveling compound. This is also the best way to smooth small ridges. Work with small quantities at a time and smooth the surface with a steel float.

Filling holes

1 Isolated holes or dips can be filled with cement mortar. Apply a concrete sealant to the sides of the hole first, to give it tooth. Concrete sealant can also be applied over an entire concrete floor to prevent it from dusting.

2 Use a flooring trowel to get the repair as smooth as possible. Once dry, any remaining bumps or ridges can be rubbed down with a carborundum block.

Correcting uneven boards

1 Use masonite to cover uneven boards. Lay the sheets flat for 48 hours in the room to acclimatize to the humidity levels. Nail them, rough side up (to give tooth for adhesives), at 6-inch intervals, using special masonite nails, in a pyramid sequence to prevent the sheet from rippling or bulging.

2 For a more solid base, use ¼-inch plywood. For soft floor coverings, allow for access to any underlying pipes and wiring before laying large sheets and make sure no nailheads protrude above the surface that will soon mar the look of the final floor. Heavy materials, such as mosaic or tile, may need a thicker base made from ½ inch exterior grade or treated marine plywood, which will not absorb water from the adhesive or grout.

Replacing boards

1 To remove a damaged straight-edged board, cut across each end just before the underlying joist (indicated by nail heads). Use a bolster chisel to lever up the board and prize out the nails. To lift tongue-and-groove boards, first chop through the tongues between two boards using the chisel and a mallet, or saw them off using a hand-held circular saw, but you will need to check first on the location of below-floor pipework and cabling.

2 Inserting a piece of wood, then pressing hard on the loose end of the board will lift the nails farther along the board.

3 Screw a batten to the side of the joist. The top edge must be hard up against the underside of the adjacent boards. Then screw down a new piece of board to the batten.

Filling gaps

Any gaps in otherwise good floorboards can be filled by tapping in wood fillets coated with adhesive. For small gaps, papier-mâché or wood putty may suffice. If the floor is to be stained or painted, such fillers will be virtually invisible.

Measuring up

Accurate measurement is essential when ordering new floor coverings. Buying a new floor—especially if you are choosing a natural material—represents one of the biggest investments you will make in your home and it is important to get it right. Most people are concerned about underestimating the amount of flooring they require; in fact, overordering is far more common and results in unnecessary waste and expense.

Start by making a scale plan of the area in question and draw it on graph paper, marking the position of doorways, windows, fireplaces, alcoves, curves, or any other irregularities of contour: rooms are rarely perfectly true in shape. A scale of 1:20 will provide enough detail.

If you do not feel confident about taking the measurements yourself, or if need to estimate a particularly awkward-shaped room or area, take your scale plan when you place your order with the flooring store. Many retailers, suppliers, and fitters offer a free service and can advise on the quantities you will need, position of seams, and so on.

Estimating unit quantities For types of flooring sold in units, find out in what dimensions the material is sold. If you intend to use 10-inch square tiles, for example, divide the total floor area by the area of one tile to calculate the total number of tiles (plus a 5% waste allowance). The same applies to boards, woodstrip, stone slabs, bricks, etc. Some mass-market flooring is sold in packs, with each pack covering a specified area. In this case, simply divide the total floor area by the area covered by each pack to determine how many packs you need.

tread

riser

Estimating for stairs
To calculate the length of a flight of stairs, run a piece of string from the top, down the risers and over the treads, to the foot. Measure the width of each tread to find the widest point of the staircase. Allow an extra 2 feet so the carpet can be turned to even out wear. If at all possible, avoid a seam at the top of the staircase, which could catch heels and be a safety hazard.

Estimating for carpet
Carpets are normally sold in standard widths. Check the roll width of your preferred carpet before estimating how much you will need. It would be costly and wasteful to buy so-called broadloom carpet for a small space or narrow room. If, on the other hand, your room or open-plan area is wider than the standard rolls available, seams are unavoidable, but there are ways of minimizing their impact. Plain carpet is more economical to fit than patterned ones, but the seams could be more apparent. Before ordering the amount you think you need, consider which is the best way for the rolls to run. In practical terms, you will want to lay carpet in whichever way requires the fewest number of strips. But there are other factors to consider. Running the strips at right angles to the main source of daylight will visually minimize the seams. Laying carpet in the same direction as the general traffic movement will mean you get the best wear from the covering. A carpet with a regular pattern may look better running with the length of the room. If you are estimating for patterned carpet, allow one matching repeat per strip in the calculations.

Calculating surface area
Multiply the width of the room by the length. To lay carpet or sheet flooring seamlessly, measure between the points of maximum width and length; for other types of flooring, work out the area of the space without its irregularities, then add in the area of alcoves or subtract the area of built-in fixtures. Add 5% extra for wastage. If the sheet or carpet is not available in rolls wide enough to cover the floor without seams, take your plan to the supplier or fitter who will be able to figure out where the seams should go.

Preparing wood

Whatever finish you intend for a wooden floor, the surface must be thoroughly prepared. It is rare to find a floor that needs only cleaning and sanding by hand: most will have years of dirt, old paint, or polish to be removed, as well as any imperfections, to reveal the glory of the wood grain again. Renting mechanical stripping equipment is usually the best way to tackle the job.

Do not underestimate the scale of the task. You will need several days to complete the job—make sure you rent all the equipment for long enough. Most jobs require a drum floor sander, an edge sander, and possibly a small disk sander, plus sheets of sandpaper to fit around the drum, in coarse, medium, and fine grits. Machine sanding is physically strenuous, dusty, and noisy. Warn the neighbors about the noise and if anyone in your family has respiratory problems, arrange for them to stay away from the house for a few days until the dust has cleared. For your personal protection, wear a mask and goggles while sanding; ear protectors are also useful. Read the operating and safety instructions that should be supplied to you with the machinery.

Begin by clearing the room, covering what you can't remove with drop cloths. Seal off doorways with plastic sheets and open windows. Cover computers and other sensitive electronic equipment elsewhere in the house.

Preparing for sanding

1 Whether or not the wood has been previously exposed, it is likely that some nails will have worked their way to the surface. Use a nail punch to sink the nail heads well below the surface and fill the holes with wood filler.

2 Tackle old paint splashes with a chemical stripper and a scraper, or sand-paper. If the floor has been painted previously, strip off as much paint as possible with a chemical stripper, or the paint will clog up the sanding sheet. Wash the floor with hot water and detergent, but avoid overwetting it.

Machine sanding

1 Try to keep the cord over your shoulder and fit the plug into a circuit breaker. Keep the sander moving – don't dwell on one spot or it will gouge a hole. If boards are very uneven, dished, or stained, sand diagonally using a coarse-grit sheet.

3 Check before sanding parquet, block, or strip floors that they are either solid wood or that the veneer is thick enough to be sanded. If you are sanding herringbone parquet, work in both directions, following the pattern, using first medium- and then fine-grit sheets.

2 Repeat the diagonal
sanding in the other
direction, always keeping
the sander moving.
This two-stage treatment
should remedy the worst
of the unevenness or
staining before you start
to smooth the surface
running parallel with
the boards.

3 Floors in better condition
can be sanded first with
medium- then fine-grit
sheets, working parallel
with the grain. Change
the sheets as needed, as
the manufacturer
instructs, and empty
the dust bag frequently.
Dispose of the sawdust
safely: it is flammable.
Never burn sawdust or
leave it lying in trash bags
in the home as it can
spontaneously combust.

4 Finish all floors by
sanding the edges with
an edge sander, first with
a medium-grit disk, then
with a fine disk. Work into
the corners and around
pipework and other
obstacles using a disc
sander, if necessary.

5 Once you have finished
sanding, wipe, sweep, or
vacuum up all remaining
dust. Give the floor a final
clean with mineral spirit
and let it dry. Despite all
your precautions, plenty of
dust has probably reached
other rooms. You will need
to vacuum walls and dust
all surfaces thoroughly.
It may take a few days for
the dust to settle.

Decorative treatments for wood

A newly stripped wooden floor can lend itself to a number of treatments using stain and varnish or paint. Whatever treatment you choose, the bare floor must be free of dust or grease, and any knots treated with knotting solution. If you intend painting the floor, it must first be primed, unless you are opting for a pickled finish. Staining needs no priming—the stain is intended to soak into the wood—but it does need good natural light to show it to its best effect. Make swatches of the paint or stain you intend to use on scraps of wood, with several coats of varnish on top, and look at them in the room to see how the light affects them.

Do not underestimate the length of time it takes to complete a decorated floor, particularly an allover treatment. You may not be able to walk over it, or move back furniture, for a few days. Several coats of paint may be required, and you must allow sufficient drying time between each coat. If you are using a stain or dye, keeping the grain of the wood apparent, one coat may be all you need, but a number of coats of sealant needed for a hardwearing finish.

Applying allover stain
Stain or dye is simple to apply. Work evenly, in the direction of the run of the boards, to keep the stain from becoming patchy.

Pickling

1 Begin by opening the grain of the wood by scrubbing it parallel with the boards with a stiff wire brush. This allows the pickling agent to sink into the grain: it is a good way of giving new boards a weathered look.

2 Use a pad of steel wool to work the pickling agent into the grain. White paint, a commercial pickling wax, or gesso will work. The wood can also be bleached or stained before pickling.

3 Use a soft, lint-free cloth to take off any surplus white from the surface.

4 The pickled floor can be waxed for a soft look or sealed with polyurethane or a similar sealant for a tough finish.

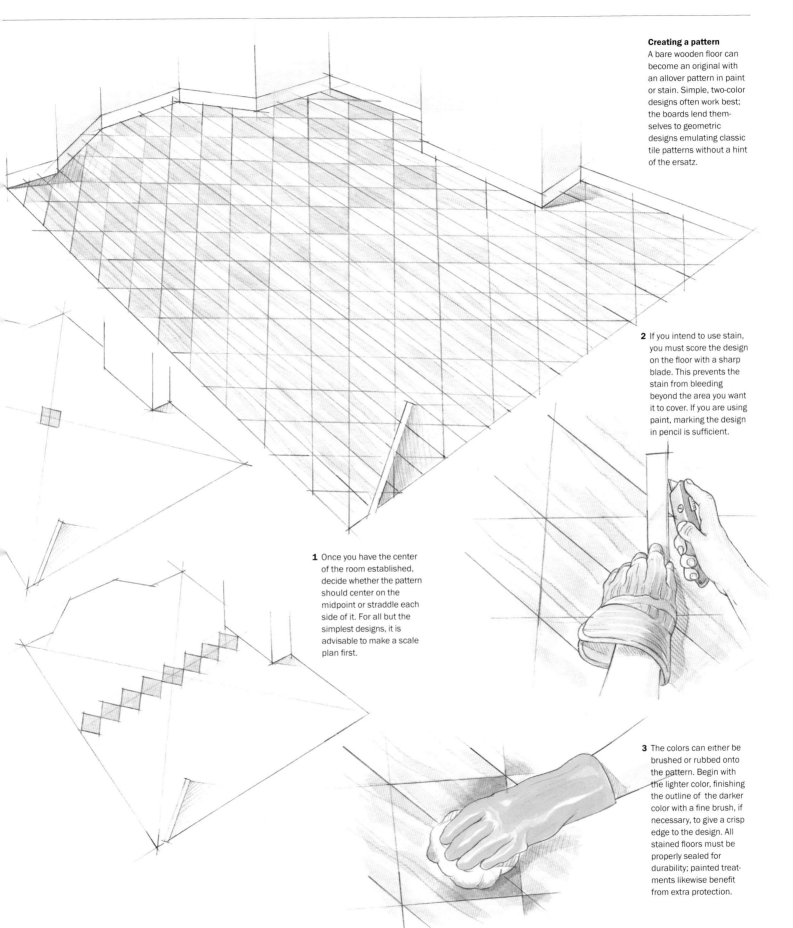

Creating a pattern
A bare wooden floor can become an original with an allover pattern in paint or stain. Simple, two-color designs often work best; the boards lend themselves to geometric designs emulating classic tile patterns without a hint of the ersatz.

2 If you intend to use stain, you must score the design on the floor with a sharp blade. This prevents the stain from bleeding beyond the area you want it to cover. If you are using paint, marking the design in pencil is sufficient.

1 Once you have the center of the room established, decide whether the pattern should center on the midpoint or straddle each side of it. For all but the simplest designs, it is advisable to make a scale plan first.

3 The colors can either be brushed or rubbed onto the pattern. Begin with the lighter color, finishing the outline of the darker color with a fine brush, if necessary, to give a crisp edge to the design. All stained floors must be properly sealed for durability; painted treatments likewise benefit from extra protection.

Stenciling, spattering, combing

Stenciling a border gives a unified, finished look that works well in the right context. The hand-done effect is part of the charm: it can give an otherwise plain wood floor a quaint, personalized quality. Suitable paints include Japan color, acrylics, poster, and oil-based paints. Aerosol paints can be used, but they are difficult to control and mean large areas must be masked off. Subtle areas of color often work better than solid bold ones.

Spattering and combing effects represent a complete departure from the grain and tones of the wood, and some interesting trompe l'oeil effects can easily be achieved by the amateur. Spattering techniques range from flecking one or more colors of paint from a stiff brush to produce a random speckled effect, to a more "mineralized" look produced by flecking mineral spirits or water over wet paint, which produces a pleasing, pebblelike finish. Combing, as the term implies, is paint applied with a wide-toothed comb either following the grain of the boards, in squares, or at random.

With all these treatments, it is vital to practice on paper or scraps of wood to gain confidence and to try out different colors and effects before tackling the floor itself. All paint effects must be covered with several coats of a transparent sealer.

Planning a border

1 If the stencil has symmetry, begin working from the center of a focal point, such as a bay window or chimney, on the wall where the design is going to be most obvious. Ending behind a door is the best way to adjust the pattern if it doesn't quite finish evenly.

2 Whether you make or buy a stencil, make sure it is made of good-quality material. Choose a pattern that is unfussy. Its size and design should help you decide how far from the room's perimeter to paint the border.

3 Make sure there is enough solid space between the cutouts so the design remains distinct as you paint through the holes. Position the stencil equidistantly each time: use the floorboards as a guide. The final effect will look more planned.

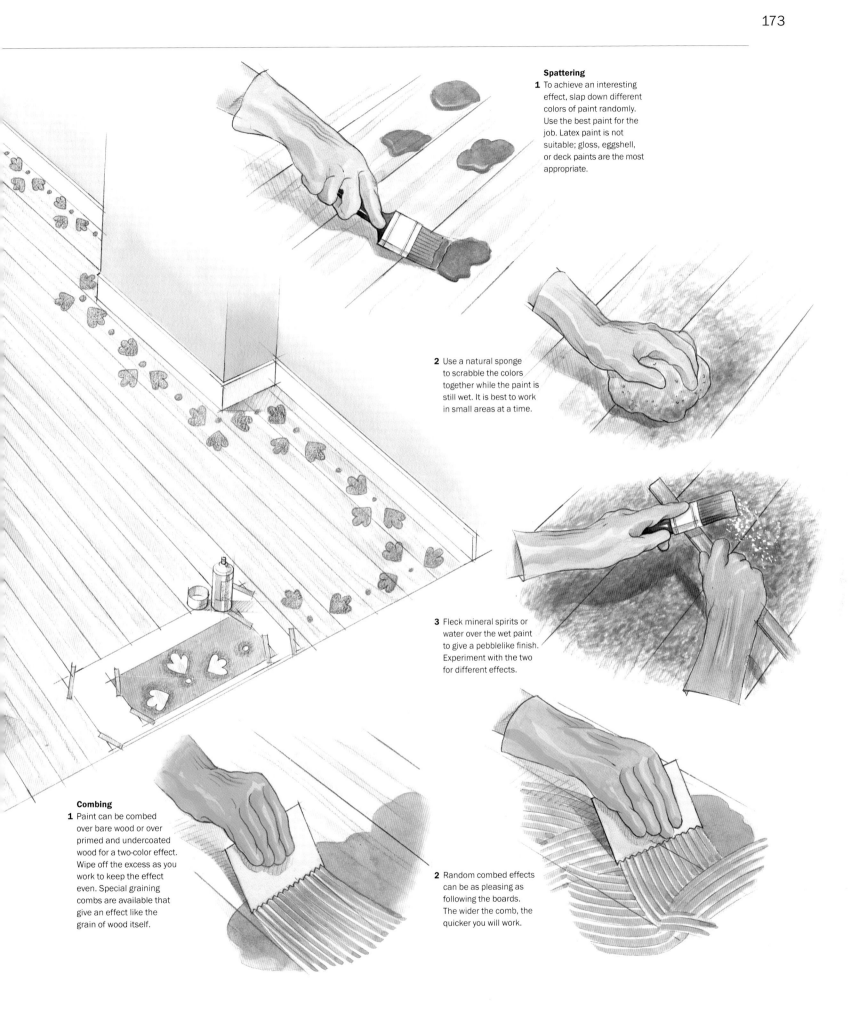

Spattering

1 To achieve an interesting effect, slap down different colors of paint randomly. Use the best paint for the job. Latex paint is not suitable; gloss, eggshell, or deck paints are the most appropriate.

2 Use a natural sponge to scrabble the colors together while the paint is still wet. It is best to work in small areas at a time.

3 Fleck mineral spirits or water over the wet paint to give a pebblelike finish. Experiment with the two for different effects.

Combing

1 Paint can be combed over bare wood or over primed and undercoated wood for a two-color effect. Wipe off the excess as you work to keep the effect even. Special graining combs are available that give an effect like the grain of wood itself.

2 Random combed effects can be as pleasing as following the boards. The wider the comb, the quicker you will work.

Laying woodblock and woodstrip

Laying a new wooden floor is a fairly straightforward project. Manufactured woodblocks and strips, either tongue and groove or straight edged, are widely available and can be laid directly onto a solid or suspended floor, provided it is dry, stable, and even. A concrete floor may need a moisture barrier. The condition of existing floorboards will affect your choice: if they are sound, you can lay woodblock directly on top, anchored either by "secret nailing," where brads are driven diagonally through the side of the blocks into the floor below, or, simpler, by gluing the blocks, which cuts down on creaks. Many are sold tongued and grooved, and can be laid as a floating floor, where only the perimeter blocks are fixed to the underlying surface. If the existing boards are not sound, you will need to take them up completely and opt for woodstrip, which is laid directly over the joists.

Laying woodblock

1 If you are covering old floorboards, plane off any unevenness before laying new blocks.

2 Apply a recommended adhesive to the underlying surface. Try to keep the amount you apply even, and cover only a small area at a time.

3 Start laying the new blocks from one corner, at right angles to the underlying boards. Plan the pattern the blocks create from the outset: staggering the seams, like rows of bricks, is usually the most stable and aesthetically pleasing.

Laying woodstrip
Woodstrip can be laid directly onto joists. The tongue-and-groove version is the easiest and quickest to lay, and gives a seamless finish.

Laying straight-edged floorboards
Unlike tongue-and-groove boards, straight-edged ones must be nailed onto the joists. Aim to vary where joined boards fall to avoid creating a line across the boards which will visually spoil the finished floor.

Allowing for expansion

All wood flooring absorbs moisture from the atmosphere, which is why it must be bought in advance and stored, free of its wrapping for at least 48 hours in the room where it is to be laid. You must allow a half-inch gap around all the walls to take into account the subsequent slight expansion of solid wood during damp weather. Purists may want to remove the baseboards and reposition them so that they sit above the expansion gap, but variously shaped wood moldings can be attached to the lower edge of the baseboards to cover the gap comfortably. A cheaper alternative is to fill in the gap with cork strip, which must be the same thickness as the new wood itself.

Filling the expansion gap
Unless you decide to remove the baseboards before laying new floorboards, use a scrap of board to gauge the expansion gap, which can be filled with cork strip (right) or covered with molding at the edge of the baseboard (see inset detail).

Laying soft tiles and sheet flooring

Soft tiles and sheet flooring materials are reasonably straightforward to lay. The technique for laying vinyl, linoleum, cork, rubber, and carpet tiles is the same. The only difference may be which adhesive to use, but many are self-adhesive. The format of tiles makes them easier to fit than sheeting, but it is important to spend some time deciding how best to lay them, usually working from the center of the room out, though not necessarily the true center. For a neat and professional finish, the trick is to avoid having an overly narrow border of cut tiles around the perimeter, which looks stingy and awkward.

Large rolls of sheet flooring, such as vinyl or linoleum, are more difficult to handle. Get someone to help you at this stage. Decide whether it would be easier to remove doors first, in order to get the sheet down with ease. You'll need to cut it roughly to size (allowing a trimming margin of at least 6 inches on all sides), then make cuts at the corners so that it can be laid flat. Then stand back to judge whether the sheet is straight, especially if it has a pattern.

Cushioned vinyl and some "stay-flat" sheets do not need to be stuck down except at the edges and along any seams. For both tiles and sheet flooring, it may be worth using a floor roller to guarantee a perfectly flat finish.

Laying vinyl tiles

1 To avoid an awkward border, calculate the center of the room (see page 166), and lay tiles loose in one of the four quarters, working away from the center point.

2 Once you have loose-laid one segment with whole tiles, check the gap that remains between the last whole tile and the perimeter of the room. If the gap is less than half a tile, adjust the true center point and loose-lay the tiles again until you find the position that means the final row of tiles will be at least half a tile. Visually, whether or not the tiles have a pattern, this looks far neater than working from the true center of the room and ending up with a very narrow final row of cut tiles at the edges.

Tiling corners

1 Position one tile on top of the last whole tile, place another tile on top, butted up against the baseboard, and then mark out where they overlap.

2 Repeat the exercise for cutting the same tile to fit around the other side of the corner so that only one whole tile is cut to fit around the angle.

Tiling round obstacles

1 It is worth making a paper pattern (left) to create the outline of any curved obstacles. You may need more than one attempt to get it right. Then transfer the image onto the tile itself for cutting (right).

2 Transfer the template to the tile and draw the cutting line on the tile before carefully cutting it.

Joining sheet flooring

To make a seam, overlap the two sheets by at least an inch—more if there is a pattern to match. Then cut through both layers. This gives a perfect seam, which can be backed with double-sided tape.

Getting a sheet straight

You will need to make cuts at all corners so that the sheet can be laid completely flat. Before cutting more accurately, check from the main doorway that the sheeting is straight.

Laying foam-backed carpet

Laying foam-backed carpet is within the scope of most home repair enthusiasts because, unlike fabric-backed carpet, it does not have to be stretched or gripped, nor does it need a separate underlay. Foam-backed carpet can be glued down or, for cheaper, quicker results, stapled or tacked, although this does not give such a neat finish. If you are laying over floorboards, put down a paper underlay, which prevents dirt from blowing up between the boards and accumulating under the carpet where it could cause damage. Masonite over uneven boards makes a good smooth surface. Concrete floors, provided they are perfectly dry, need no such underlay.

Unless you are confident, start with a small room before tackling a large area. If there are obstacles, say, a sink pedestal, it is best to make a pattern by covering the floor with paper, leaving a small margin, and using a pen held against a small block to scribe around the perimeter. For less awkward jobs or large surfaces, it is adequate to cut the carpet roughly to size, allowing approximately 6 inches for trimming on all sides. Keep some of the waste: it may be useful for patching later.

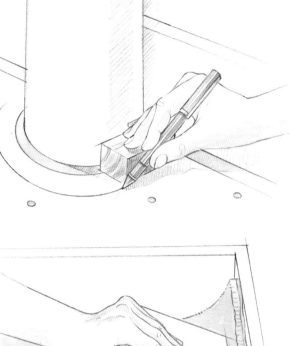

Making a paper pattern
Use a small block of wood to scribe around an obstacle, marking the outlines exactly on the paper. Then lay the pattern on the carpet, right side up, and use the same block of wood to retrace the outline onto the carpet itself.

Laying the carpet

1 If you need to join two pieces of carpet, the seam can be secured with double-sided tape. Additional strips of tape may also be needed across the width of the room to hold the carpet in position.

2 Use a straight-edged board to butt the carpet up to the baseboard.

3 Trim away any surplus, cutting against the edge of the baseboard with a sharp knife. Make sure your free hand is protected with a sturdy glove: it is all too easy for the knife to slip.

4 Fold back the carpet over a board to cut neatly to fit a corner or alcove. This will avoid the risk of damaging the surface of the carpet itself as you work in an awkward space.

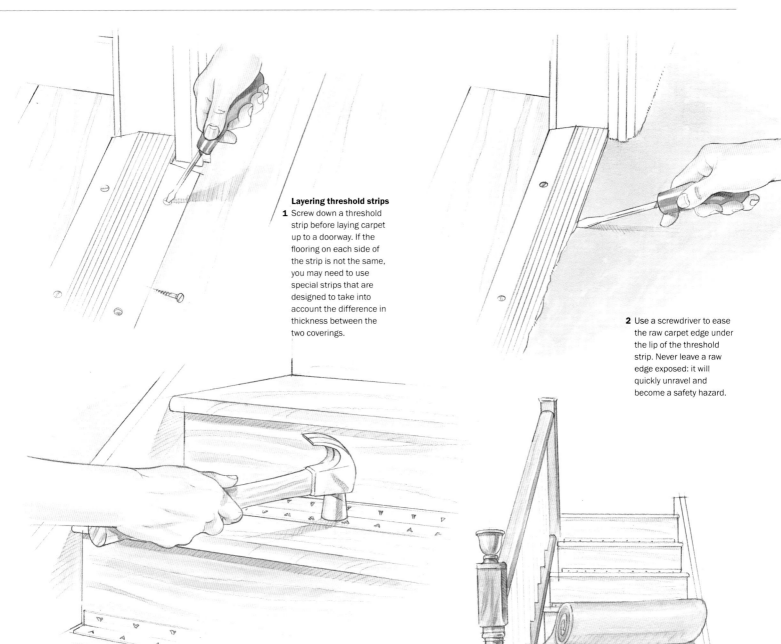

Layering threshold strips

1 Screw down a threshold strip before laying carpet up to a doorway. If the flooring on each side of the strip is not the same, you may need to use special strips that are designed to take into account the difference in thickness between the two coverings.

2 Use a screwdriver to ease the raw carpet edge under the lip of the threshold strip. Never leave a raw edge exposed: it will quickly unravel and become a safety hazard.

Carpeting stairs

If you have straight stairs, you may feel confident enough to lay fabric-backed carpet, because the narrow width means the roll is far less heavy and unwieldy than, say, a roll of broadloom for carpeting a large area. Standard-width stair carpet is available, and there are special angled grippers that fit at the junction between tread and riser. The carpet is stretched over the stairs and onto a gripper strip so that it catches on the angled teeth. It takes strength and skill to stretch the carpet tightly over the grippers. Begin at the foot of the stairs, pushing the roll up the stairs as you work. Make sure you avoid a seam at the top of the stairs, which could be hazardous. Aim to make the seam at least 2 feet away from the top step, so that in time the carpet can be lifted and turned to even out wear. Alternatively, make the seam meet under the lip of the top stair, where it won't catch heels.

Maintenance

Your decision when choosing a flooring material should in part be influenced by the maintenance required once a floor is laid. You need to have an idea of how much effort (and possible expense) you are prepared to devote to its care and whether your choice is sensible, given the location for which it is intended. Different materials require cleaning in different ways, and you should always use products and techniques recommended by the suppliers or manufacturers to give a long life for the floor. This final section gives an indication of the ease—or otherwise—of maintaining all the flooring materials discussed in the book.

Hard floors

Brick

Make sure any mortar residue is cleaned from a new brick floor immediately after laying, all to prevent staining. Commercial cleansers are available for this task. Once laid, bricks generally need little in the way of aftercare. They can be polished, dressed with linseed oil, or sealed—sparingly (sealant is not recommended at all for absorbent bricks), but none of these treatments is necessary and can increase the slipperiness of the surface. You will need to remove any old polish completely from time to time to prevent a buildup of dirt. General maintenance of a brick floor is very simple: it consists of sweeping regularly, washing with a mild detergent, and rinsing thoroughly with clean water.

Stone

Most limestone and sandstone are porous and stain readily. Sealing will prevent staining but is not always recommended, and it can alter the appearance of the floor. Never polish smooth-textured stone, which will make it dangerously slippery.

To clean stone floors, wash with warm water and a noncaustic, sulfatefree detergent, then rinse. Never use alkaline soap on marble; it will corrode the surface irreparably. Specialist cleaning may be required for stubborn stains. Antique stone reclaimed from old houses may need to be steam-pressure cleaned.

Hard tiles

Porous tiles (terra cotta, quarry, and encaustic) need to be sealed to inhibit staining using a commercial sealer or a dressing of two coats of beeswax mixed with boiled linseed oil. Sealing needs to be carried out before the tiles are laid and again after grouting. The seal must be applied to completely clean and dry tiles; otherwise, moisture and dirt will be trapped in the tiles. Apply a light, even coat of seal so that it doesn't dry in streaks or blotches.

General maintenance is straightforward: wash with warm water and a mild detergent and rinse thoroughly. Any white patches appearing on porous tiles are the result of salt deposits in the tiles: further washing with clean water shouldbe enough. A wax paste applied to thoroughly dry tiles gives a final finish. Apply two or three coats after sealing, then weekly for the first six weeks to create a hard-wearing surface.

Mop up spills as soon as possible using a soft cloth and clean water. Acidic liquids, including citrus juices, soft drinks, alcohol, vinegar, and urine, are liable to cause stains, especially on tiles that are unsealed. Try using mineral spirits to lift the more stubbon marks.

Glazed tiles need no sealing. Wash with a gentle detergent and rinse. If you wish to polish the tiles, use only small amounts, renewed from time to time. Dirty grout can be cleaned with a commercial tile bleach.

To restore an old encaustic floor, use a floor scrubber to lift out dirt, and steel wool to work into the corners. Encaustic tiles stain easily before they are sealed and should be handled with care.

Terrazzo and mosaic

The smooth surface of terrazzo is fairly non-slip, except when wet, washed with soap, or polished. General maintenance is simple: wash regularly with a little scouring powder and rinse with clean water. Avoid using a polish that contains wax, which will make the surface too slippery.

Mosaic needs washing with a gentle detergent. Never apply a high polish, or the natural key provided by the difference in texture between mosaic and grouting will be lost and the surface will be dangerously slippery.

Concrete, metal, and glass

Concrete floors must be sealed to prevent the surface from dusting. Once sealed, maintain by scrubbing with hot water and a gentle detergent. Metal and glass are cleaned in the same way, too. Make sure that any glass surfaces are thoroughly dry before walking over them.

Wood

Properly sealed (see page 100) and finished, wood is straightforward to keep clean on a regular basis. Wax polishes will need to be renewed every couple of months, but most seals will last far longer and can be patch repaired in areas which are most heavily used. Vacuum or sweep up loose dirt and wipe the surface with a damp cloth or mop. Avoid overwetting the floor.

Despite being fairly low maintenance on a regular bais, wooden floors demand more in the long term. Once the seal has begun to wear all over, it must be replaced before dirt and moisture can penetrate the wood and begin to degrade it. Really worn floors may need refinishing (see pages 168–69).

Avoid spike heels at all costs, even at the risk of embarassing your guests! There is no quicker or more effective way of ruining any kind of wood floor than to subject it to the type of intense point load exerted by high heels. The marks not only break the seal, but leave lasting dents that can only be eradicated by deep sanding (which would be impossible on a wood veneer floor).

Sheet and soft tiling

Cork

Cork needs to be sealed to protect it from soiling and to make it water-resistant. Presealed cork can be given an extra coat of seal after laying to prevent moisture from penetrating joints. Alternatively, unsealed cork can be wax-polished or dressed with organic primers. Cork flooring with a vinyl finish is much more resistant and requires no subsequent treatment. Seals and polishes should be renewed as soon as they show signs of wear. Cork can be lightly sanded if the surface has become pitted or soiled. It will gradually fade a little in strong sunlight. Natural cork is also very susceptible to cigarette burns and alkaline chemicals.

A cork floor demands dedicated upkeep to preserve its appearance. It is important to make sure the cork is kept clean and free from grit which might break down the seal and allow dirt and moisture through. Sweep or vacuum regularly, wipe with a damp cloth, and polish occasionally and sparingly. Spills must be mopped up immediately.

Rubber

Natural rubber is readily marked by fats and solvents, but even synthetic rubber can be damaged if it is left unpolished. Use polish sparingly and renew it from time to time.

Clean the floor regularly with a mild detergent. Go over the surface with a damp mop rinsed out in clear water to remove all traces of detergent, which otherwise might leave a residue. Take care with a rubber floor that has a smooth finish: the surface can be very slippery when wet.

Linoleum

Linoleum needs no sealing, but buffing it with an emulsion polish can bring up a glossy sheen. Before polishing, allow up to 48 hours after laying to give the adhesive time to cure.

For regular maintenance, dust mop or vacuum to remove loose grit and dirt which can scratch the surface and use a damp mop with a mild detergent on soiled floors. Avoid overwetting the floor. Strip off the polish occasionally with a recommended stripper and renew. Mop up spills as soon as they occur. Linoleum resists most stains, but solvents such as gasoline,, drycleaning fluid, nail polish and nail polish remover, washing soda, and oven cleaner can do lasting damage. Cigarette burns can be rubbed or buffed away.

Vinyl

Vinyl is waterproof and resistant to oils, fats, and most household chemicals, which is why it is such an easy-care, all-purpose flooring for hardworking areas of the home, although smooth vinyl is slippery when wet.

However, unlike natural materials, which may mellow with time, worn vinyl is merely shoddy. For this reason, you must make sure that the right cleaning products are used and that the floor is protected from the type of spills most likely to damage it, as well as from grit, which will rapidly wear the surface. Black rubber heel marks can be particularly detrimental; if not tackled immediately, antioxidants in the rubber can stain the material permanently. Rubber-backed rugs and mats can result in similar problems. Premature damage will also be caused by the use of the wrong cleaners, such as bleach, scouring powder, liquid-based abrasives, and strong alkaline detergents. Permanent damage or staining can be caused by spike heels, hot objects, cigarette burns, road tar, citrus juices or syrup, gasoline, kerosene, mineral spirits, bleach, drycleaning fluid, nail polish remover, paint stripper, acids generally, and certain hair preparations.

Cushioned vinyl is particularly likely to be damaged by moving heavy objects, such as household appliances, over the floor. To protect the surface, place a piece of carpet underneath the appliance so that it can be pushed or pulled across the floor; alternatively "walk" the appliance over a sheet of plywood.

For general maintenance, wash with a damp mop and neutral or mild detergent. Rinse thoroughly to avoid a buildup of detergent, which might dull the surface. Avoid overwetting the floor.

Polish vinyl with a water-wax emulsion polish. Do not use polish containing solvents. Sweep or vacuum regularly, because grit will abrade the surface of the material and cause it to wear through. If vinyl is laid in halls or entranceways, make sure you provide a doormat across the full width to remove loose dirt and debris, but choose one that is not latex or rubber-backed as the rubber can stain.

Leather

To protect and enrich leather, the newly laid floor should be waxed and buffed at least three times before you walk on it. Subsequently, buff the floor every two weeks and wax it about twice a year.

Waxing provides basic moisture-resistance, and spills, if tackled immediately, will wipe off. Scratches are inevitable, but add to the character; a well-used floor has great depth of appeal.

Soft floors

Carpet

New carpet sheds a great deal of fluff in the first few weeks. During this period, it is best not to vacuum or to subject the floor to heavy wear. When the carpet has settled down, vacuum at least once a week. In areas where traffic is heaviest, more frequent vacuuming may be necessary. Animal hairs can be particularly tenacious: work slowly over the area, using a stiff brush as well if necessary.

Like any textile, carpet does stain. Stain-inhibition treatments, which may be either integral or applied after the carpet is laid, will only minimize damage, not entirely prevent it. Tackle spills immediately. Blot liquids with a damp cloth or paper towel to get as much off the surface as possible before the spill has a chance to be absorbed into the pile. Scrape up more solid deposits with a blunt knife. Do not add any additional liquid or you will spread the stain. After you have cleared or blotted as much as you can, wash the area gently, working from the outer rim of the stain to the center. Do not scrub or you may damage the fibers and force the stain down into the pile. Avoid overwetting at all costs.

Stain treatment depends on whether the stain is water- or oil-based. For water-based stains, use a gentle cleaning solution made from warm water and a dash of mild liquid detergent (such as a wool detergent, or carpet shampoo). For oil-based stains use drycleaning fluid or solvent. Dampen a cloth with the cleaning solution and dab the stain, working from the outside in. Blot to dry.

Stain checklist:

Alcohol—Blot and wash with detergent. Never apply salt to wine stains
Blood—Blot and wash with a cold-water detergent solution
Burn—Cut off burned fibers and wash with detergent
Chewing gum—Freeze with ice wrapped in plastic, scrape off, and clean with drycleaning fluid
Coffee—Blot and wash with detergent. When dry, use drycleaning fluid to take out grease from milk or cream.
Egg—Scrape off and clean with drycleaning fluid

Fats and oils—Blot or scrape, as appropriate, and clean with drycleaning fluid
Grass—Clean with drycleaning fluid
Ink—Blot and wash with detergent or clean with drycleaning fluid, depending on type
Juice—Blot and wash with detergent
Milk—Blot and wash with detergent. When dry, clean with drycleaning fluid
Mud—Let it dry, then vacuum or brush up dirt. Wash with detergent
Paint—Scrape and then wash with detergent (water-based paint) or clean with drycleaning fluid (oil-based paint)
Shoe polish—Scrape and clean with drycleaning fluid
Tar—Scrape and clean with drycleaning fluid
Tea—Blot and wash with detergent. When dry, clean with drycleaning fluid to remove grease from milk.
Urine—Blot, wash with detergent with a dash of antiseptic
Vomit—Scrape, wash with detergent with a dash of antiseptic
Wax—Scrape, applying mild heat to soften, then clean with drycleaning fluid

Once a year carpets can be shampooed using a commercial dry foam shampoo: follow the instructions and do not overwet. For a more thorough overhaul, it may be worth calling in professional carpet cleaners. Such firms use wet vacuum cleaners to spray jets of cleaning solution into the pile. Carpets can take up to a day to dry after this treatment.

Natural fiber coverings

Many natural fibers are susceptible to wear from castors, so it is best to have additional protection under heavy furniture and chair and sofa legs. High, spike heels are also best avoided. Bright sunshine may cause fading in some varieties. Many of them, with the exception of rush, react differently and usually adversely to humidity. Coir expands with moisture and may wrinkle and buckle. As it dries out, joints may open up. Sisal, on the other hand, shrinks when wet. In very damp conditions, all natural fibers rot.

For regular maintenance, all of these floorings should be vacuumed. Never wash or shampoo. Coir, sisal, and jute are best treated with a stain-inhibition treatment. Tackle spills immediately, blotting up as much as possible from the surface before staining has a chance to occur. Let muddy tracks dry out, then brush along the grain and vacuum.

Rugs

Like carpets, rugs should be vacuumed regularly to remove dirt and debris which might degrade the pile. Vacuum gently in the direction of the pile, avoiding the fringe. Sweep fringe gently with a brush.

Sources

Hard Floors

Brick, stone, terrazzo, tiles (ceramic, encaustic, quarry, terra-cotta), mosaic, concrete, metal.

American Marazzi Tile
359 Clay Road
Sunnyvale, TX 75182
972-226-0110
Glazed tiles, high-slip resistance. Informational brochure.

Arizona Tile
1245 W. Elliot St., #111
Tempe, AZ 85284
602-940-9555
Marble flooring. Informational brochures on various types of flooring available.

Country Floors
15 East 16th Street
New York, NY 10003
212-627-8300
American and imported ceramics and terra-cottas. Special-order tiles. Catalog.

Dal–Tile Corp.
7834 Hawn Freeway
Dallas, TX 75217
800-933-TILE
Assorted tiles. Catalog

Fired Earth Tiles PLC
Twyford Mill
Oxford Road
Adderbury, Oxon
OX17 3HP
England
(44) 129-581-2088
Natural floor coverings, ceramic tile, marble, granite. Worldwide delivery. Catalog

Imperial Black Marble Co.
P.O. Box 103
Thorn Hill, TN 37881
423-767-2888
Sequoyah light rose and black marble flooring. Sells mostly wholesale, but will sell retail. Custom and historical-detail work. Samples available.

Muirfield ICI Ceramics, Inc.
55 Route One South
Iselin, NJ 08830
908-855-1100
Custom and production ceramic tiles for floors and other uses. Catalog.

Native Tiles and Ceramics
Diana & Tom Watson
4230 Glencoe Avenue
Marina Del Rey, CA 90292
310-823-8684
Reproduction tiles. Catalog.

Paris Ceramics
979 Third Avenue
New York, NY 10022
888-845-3487
Limestone, terra-cotta, antique stone, and hand-painted tiles. Catalog. Call for nearest retailer.

Summitville Tiles
P.O. Box 73
Summitville, OH 43962
330-223-1511
Imperva-mates™ glazed mosaic. Catalog.

Through Tiles
145 Hudson Street
4th Floor
New York, NY 10013
212-255-4450
Pyrolave™ (cut from sheets of dry lava) flooring material and counter tops. Catalog $20.

The Tile Studio
Bruno Haase
1 Lansdowne Avenue
Merrick, NY 11566
516-623-2600
Custom and production ceramic tiles for floors and other uses. Catalog.

Wooden Floors

Both new timber of various kinds and suppliers of renovated old floorboards.

Aged Woods, Inc.
2331 East Market Street
York, PA 17402
800-233-9307
Antique heart pine, hickory, ash, and other unusual domestic flooring. Catalog.

Anderson Hardwood Flooring
P.O. Box 1155
Clinton, SC 29325
803-833-6250
Large selection of hardwood flooring. Catalog.

Authentic Pine Floors, Inc.
P.O. Box 206
Locust Grove, GA 30248
800-283-6038
Wide-plank and heart pine flooring. Catalog.

Bangkok International
4562 Worth Street
Philadelphia, PA 19124
215-537-5800
Hardwood flooring: teak, rosewood, birch, ash, mahogany, oak. Catalog.

Boen Hardwood Flooring
350 Hollie Drive
Bowels Industrial Park
Martinsville, VA 24112
540-638-3700
Various types of wood flooring.
Information packet available.

Broad-Axe Beam Co.
RD 2, P.O. Box 417
Brattleboro, VT 05301
802-257-0064
Wide pine flooring; hand-hewn
beams. Nationwide shipping.
Catalog.

Bruce Hardwood Floors
P.O. Box 660100
Dallas, TX 75248
800-535-0423
Strip, plank, parquet, wood tile,
and acrylic-impregnated
hardwood floors. Catalog.

The Burruss Company
P.O. Box 6
Brookneal, VA 24528
800-334-2495
Oak, pine, maple, ash, walnut,
and cherry floors. Catalog.

Capitol Wood Floors
143 Route 59
Hillburn, NY 10931
914-369-3738
All types of wood flooring.
Catalogs.

Carlisle Restoration Lumber
HCR 32 Box 556C
Stoddard, NH 03464-9712
800-595-9663
Eastern white pine wide-board
flooring. Nationwide delivery.
Portfolio and sample kit
available.

Craftsman Lumber Co.
P.O. Box 222
Groton, MA 01450
508-448-5621
Pine flooring, paneling, railroad
siding. Catalog.

Desoto Hardwood Flooring
Company
977 Sledge Avenue
Memphis, TN 38104
901-774-9672
Oak, maple, cherry, walnut strip
flooring. Catalog.

Diamond K. Co., Inc.
130 Buckland Road
South Windsor, CT 06074
860-644-8486
Wide-plank flooring, barn wood
beams. Catalog.

Dixon Lumber Company
P.O. Box 907
Galax, VA 24333
540-236-9963
Refinished, laminated, and
unfinished oak and maple
flooring. Catalog.

Dynamic Laser Applications
4704 Ecton Drive
Marietta, GA 30066
800-849-8575
Borders, medallions, stripwood
flooring, and wood inlays in
standard and exotic woods.
Catalog.

E.T. Moore Company
3100 North Hopkins Road
Suite 101
Richmond, VA 23224
804-231-1823
Heart pine flooring. Catalog.

Forest Stewardship Council
Avenida Hidalgo 502
Oaxaca 68000
Oaxaca
Mexico
(52) 951 46905
International body that issues a
certificate for timber from
sustainably managed forests

Guyon
Rear 20, Doe Run Road
Manhein, PA 17545
717-664-2485
Flooring, ceiling beams. Catalog.

Harris-Tarkett, Inc.
2225 Eddie Williams Rd.
Johnson City, TN 37601
800-842-7816
Hardwood flooring in many
styles and finishes, including
Quiet Core™. Catalog.
Call for nearest retailer.

Hartco/Tibbals Flooring
Company
900 S. Gay Street, Suite 2102
Knoxville, TN 37902
423-544-0767
Parquet, herringbone, and
basketweave commercial and
residential flooring. Catalog.

Historic Floors of Oshkosh
911 East Main
Winneconne, WI 54986
414-582-9977
Borders, marquees, and
medallions available in 27
types of wood. Catalog.

International Hardwood
Flooring, Inc.
7400 Edmund Street
Philadelphia, PA 19136
800-338-7481
Australian jarra, Tasmanian
oak, Brazilian cherry and
walnut, and others. Catalog.

J.L. Powell & Company, Inc.
107 Powell Bldg.
600 S. Madison
Whiteville, NC 28472
800-227-2007
Heart pine flooring. Catalog.

The Joinery Company
P.O. Box 518
Tarboro, NC 27886
800-726-7463
Factory direct: antique heart
pine flooring, millwork, raised
paneled doors, etc. Catalog.

Kentucky Wood Floors
P.O. Box 33276
Louisville, KY 40232
800-235-5235
Custom wood flooring. Catalog.

Linden Lumber Company
Dawer 480369
Linden, AL 36748
800-251-8751
Oak and pine flooring. Catalog.

Livermore Wood Floors/Wood
Mill
P.O. Box 146
East Livermore, ME 04228
207-897-5211
Cherry, oak, maple, ash, wide
pine, walnut, and birch.
Catalog.

Mannington Wood Floors
1327 Lincoln Drive
High Point, NC 27260-9945
910-884-5600
Northern red oak flooring.
Catalog.

Memphis Hardwood
Flooring Co.
P.O. Box 38217
Memphis, TN 38107
800-346-3010
Oak flooring. Catalog.

Mountain Lumber Co.
P.O. Box 289
Ruckersville, VA 22968-0289
800-445-2671
Antique heart pine flooring.
Samples available.

New England Hardwood
Supply Co.
P.O. Box 2254
Littleton, MA 01460
508-486-8683
Hardwood flooring. Catalog.

Pine Floors, Inc.
P.O. Box 206
Locust Grove, GA 30248
800-283-6038
Heart pine flooring. Catalog
available.

River City Woodworks
825 9th Street
New Orleans, LA 70115
504-899-7278
Antique pine flooring, lumber,
moldings, doors, stair parts.
Catalog.

S & S Mills
200 Howell Drive
Dalton, GA 30721
800-363-8391
Large selection of wood flooring
to order direct. Catalog.

Sullivan Floors
506 East 118th Street
New York, NY 10035
212-353-3490
All types of wood flooring.
Catalogs.

Vintage Lumber &
Construction Co.
P.O. Box 104
Woodsboro, MD 21798
800-499-7859
Antique pine and oak flooring.
Catalog.

Vintage Pine Company
P.O. Box 85
Prospect, VA 23960
804-574-6531
Heart pine flooring and
architectural components.
Catalog.

Zickgraf Hardwood Company
P.O. Box 1149
Franklin, NC 28734
800-243-1277
Oak and maple flooring.
Catalog.

Sheet and Soft Tiling
Cork, rubber, linoleum, and
vinyl.

American Floor Products Co.,
Inc.
7300 Westmore Road
Rockville, MD 20850
800-342-0424
Rubber and vinyl tile flooring
and stair treads. Catalog.

Amtico
200 Lexington Avenue
Suite 809
New York, NY 10017
800-268-4260
Luxury vinyl tile flooring and
vinyl wall base. Catalog. Call for
nearest retailer.

Armstrong World Industries
P.O. Box 3001
Lancaster, PA 17604
800-704-8000
Solarian™ floors. Catalog.

Dodge-Regupol Incorporated
P.O. Box 989
Lancaster, PA 17608-0989
800-322-1923
Natural cork floor tiles and
recycled rubber flooring.
Catalog.

Gerbert, Ltd.
P.O. Box 4944
Lancaster, PA 17604
888-359-5466
German-made linoleum sheets
and tiles. Catalog.

Home Depot
Store Support Center
2455 Paces Ferry Road
Atlanta, GA 30339-4024
800-553-3199
Vinyl and wood flooring.
Informational brochures
available. Call for nearest
retailer.

Janovic Plaza
718-786-4444
New York City- and Nassau
County, NY-based retail stores
carry a variety of vinyl tiles and
flooring materials. Informational
brochures available. Call for
store listing.

Linoleum City
5657 Santa Monica Boulevard
Hollywood, CA 90038
213-469-0063
Huge selection of linoleum
styles from period to modern to
high tech. Catalog.

Lonseal
928 East 238th Street
Building A
Carson, CA 90745
800-832-7111
Sheet vinyl flooring in 134
different styles and colors.
Catalog. Call for nearest
retailer.

National Floor Products Co.,
Inc.
P.O. Box 354
Florence, AL 35631
800-227-4662
Luxury vinyl flooring. Catalog.
Call for nearest retailer.

Tarkett, Inc.
P.O. Box 264
Parsippany, NJ 07054
201-428-9000
Vinyl and ceramic tile flooring.
Catalog.

Toli International
55 Mall Drive
Commack, NY 11725
800-446-5476
Vinyl flooring. Catalog.

Soft Floors
Natural fibers (sisal, jute, coir,
seagrass) carpets and rugs.

ABC Carpet & Home
888 Broadway
New York, NY 10003
212-473-3000
Contemporary and Oriental rugs
and carpets; natural fiber floor
coverings; small-space area
rugs. Catalog.

A Candle In The Night
181 Main Street
Brattleboro, VT 05302
802-257-0471
One-of-a-kind Oriental and
Turkish rugs. Catalog.

The Antique Guild
3231 Helms Avenue
Los Angeles, CA 90034
310-838-3131
Period and Oriental rugs.
Different catalogs available
depending on type of rug
desired.

Carpetmax Flooring Center
800-4-FLOORS
Hotline for ordering complete guide to buying carpets.

Claremont Rug Company
6087 Claremont Avenue
Oakland, CA 94618
800-441-1332
Antique art carpets. Catalog $10.

Cleopatra Steps Out
721 Cookman Avenue
Asbury Park, NJ 07712
908-774-6306
A rug design gallery featuring hand-tufted rugs designed by artists and craftspeople. Catalog.

Einstein Moomjy
150 East 58th Street
New York, NY 10022
800-864-3633C
Carries a wide variety of rugs, carpets, and dhurries. Catalogs.

Mansour
8600 Melrose Avenue
Los Angeles, CA 90069
310-652-9999
Persian, Oriental, and European rugs. Trade and retail. Catalog.

Merida Natural Fiber Flooring
P.O. Box 1071
Syracuse, NY 13201
800-345-2200
Natural fiber floors and a wide choice of unusual bindings. Catalog. Call for nearest retailer.

Rosecone Carpet Company
979 Third Avenue
New York, NY 10022
212-421-7272
Handmade Aubusson-weave rugs. Catalog. Call for nearest retailer.

The Rug Barn
P.O. Box 1187
Abbeville, SC 29620
864-446-3136
Large selection of rugs to order direct. Catalog.

Rug Oasis
115 West Avenue
Kannapolis, NC 28081
800-524-6902
Large selection of Karastan™ carpets and other brands. Catalog.

S & S Mills
200 Howell Drive
Dalton, GA 30721
800-241-4013
Large selection of rugs to order direct. Catalog.

Safavieh Carpet
153 Madison Avenue
New York, NY 10016
888-723-2843
Vegetable-dyed rugs. Catalog.

Susan Sargent Designs, Inc.
Route 30
Pawlet, VT 05761
800-245-4767
Artist-owned company creating original designs and colorful rugs. Catalog $10, applied to first order.

Miscellaneous
Rubber, leather, and other unusual materials.

Altro Floors
467 Forbes Boulevard
San Francisco, CA 94080
800-382-0333
Sheet vinyl safety flooring systems. Catalog.

Connor—AGA
251 Industrial Park Road
Amasa, MI 49903
800-833-7144
Vinyl and rubber flooring, specializing in sports and recreation. Catalog.

Endura
P.O. Box 9045
Waltham, MA 02254-9045
800-643-7463
Rubber flooring and stair treads, including for the visually impaired. Catalog. Call for nearest retailer.

Formica Corporation
10155 Reading Road
Cincinnati, OH 45241
800-367-6422
Customized laminate flooring. Catalog. Call for nearest retailer.

Granwood Flooring System
P.O. Box 910
Port Washington, NY 11050
800-544-9499
Vinyl and rubber flooring, specializing in sports and recreation. Catalog.

Mary Moross Studios
122 Chambers Street
New York, NY 10007
212-571-0437
Hand-painted, custom, and production canvas floor cloths. Catalog.

Teddy & Arthur Edelman, Ltd. (Edelman Leather)
28 Hawleyville Road
Hawleyville, CT 06440
800-886-8339
Enormous selection of quality leathers for residential and contract use, including leather floor tiles. Catalog. To the trade only.

Wilsonart International
P.O. Box 6110
Temple, TX 76503
800-710-8846
Laminated tiles that resemble stone, marble, and ceramic. Catalog. Call for nearest retailer.

Trade Associations
The following associations provide consumer brochures, videos, and information on distributors, installers, fabricators, and retailers.

California Redwood Association
405 Enfrente Drive
Suite 200
Novato, CA 94949
888-225-7339

The Carpet & Rug Institute
P.O. Box 2048
Dalton, GA 30722
706-278-3176

Ceramic Tile Institute of America
1206 Jefferson Boulevard
Culver City, CA 90230-6219
310-574-7800

Granite Industries of Vermont
P.O. Box 537
Barre, VT 05641
802-479-2202

Hardwood Manufacturers Association
400 Penn Center Building
Suite 530
Pittsburgh, PA 15235
800-373-WOOD

Maple Flooring Manufacturers Association (MFMA)
60 Revere Drive
Suite 500
Northbrook, IL 60062
708-480-9138

Marble Institute of America (MIA)
30 Eden Alley
Suite 201
Columbus, OH 43215
614-228-6194

National Oak Flooring Manufacturers Association (NOFMA)
22 North Front Street
Suite 660
Memphis, TN 38103
901-526-5016

National Wood Flooring Association (NWFA)
11046 Manchester Road
St. Louis, MO 63122
800-422-4556

Southern Pine Council
P.O. Box 641700
Kenner, LA 70064
504-443-4464

Western Wood Products Association
Yeon Building
522 Fifth Avenue
Portland, OR 97204-2122
503-224-3930

Professional Associations
The following associations can provide consumers with lists of local interior designers and architects who might specialize in flooring.

American Institute of Architects (AIA)
1735 New York Avenue, N.W.
Washington, DC 20006
202-626-7300
Search from a resource library of reputable architects at http//www.aiaonline.com.

American Society of Interior Designers (ASID)
608 Massachusetts Avenue, N.E.
Washington, DC 20002
202-546-3480
Provides a client referral line: residential, 800-775-2743; commercial, 800-610-2743.

Architects and designers whose work is featured in this book (numbers refer to pages on which their work is illustrated)

Adjaye & Russell
(26–27)
27 Sunbury Workshops
Swanfield Street
London E2 5LF
England
(44) 171-739-4969

Charlotte Barnes
(91)
26 Stanhope Gardens
London SW7 5QX
England
(44) 171-244-9610

Felix Bonnier
(67, 77, 101)
Form a
6 rue Monsigny
75002 Paris
France
(33) 1 49.26.09.83

Simon & Robyn Carnachan
(12 left)
Carnachan Architects Ltd
27 Bath Street, Parnell
P.O. Box 37-717
Auckland
New Zealand
(64) 9-3797-234

Circus Architects
(14–15, 29 right)
1a Summers Street
London EC1R 5BD
England
(44) 171-833-1999

Jacqueline Coumans
(153 above)
Le Décor Français
1006 Lexington Avenue
New York NY 10021
212-734-0032

DAD Associates
(11 right, 62–63)
112-6 Old Street
London EC1V 9BD
England
(44) 171-336-6488

Robert Dye Associates
(6–7, 18–19, 108–9)
68–74 Rochester Place
London NW1 9JX
England
(44) 171-267-9388

Amanda Freedman
(88, 89 above center and below left, 132–3), based in Notting Hill, London, England
Fax (44) 171-727-6860

Mark Guard Associates
(18 center, 29 below left, 32–33)
161 Whitfield Street
London W1P 5RY
England
(44) 171-380-1199

Hudson Featherstone
(25 below left, 30 above left, 42–43, 46–47, 78–79, 109, 136–37)
Rowland Hill House
49-59 Old Street
London EC1V 9HX
England
(44) 171-490-5656

Hilton McConnico
(34–35)
3 rue Antoine Panier
93170 Bagnolet
France
(33) 1 43.62.53.16

Interni
(22 above left, 56, 76 below left)
Interior Design Consultancy
15-19 Boundary Street
Rushcutters Bay
2011 Sydney
Australia

IPL Interiors
(48 left, 93)
François Gilles and Dominique Lubar
Unit 26C1, Thames House
140 Battersea Park Road
London SW11 4NY
England
(44) 171-622-3009

Lyn Le Grice
(98 above, 98–99 above)
Flower Loft, Treriefe
Penzance
Cornwall TR20 8TS
England
(44) 1736-364193

Khai Liew Design
(37, 55)
166 Magill Road
Norwood 50067
South Australia
(61) 8-8362-1076

MCDowell & Benedetti
(13 below right, 61, 93,
130–31)
62 Rosebery Avenue
London EC1R 4RR
England
(44) 171-278-8810

Frédéric Méchiche
(4–5, 16–17, 41, 52–52,
72–73, 87)
4 rue de Thorigny
75003 Paris
France

Paxton Locher Architects
(84–85)
8 Clerkenwell Green
London EC1R 0DE
England
(44) 171-251-6645

Pentagram Architecture
(51 below)
James Biber
204 Fifth Avenue
New York NY 10010
212-683-7071

Andrew Parr, SJB Interior
Design
(13 below left, 139 below)
P O Box 1149
South Melbourne 3205
Australia
(61) 3-9688-2122

Campion A. Platt Architect
(49)
641 Fifth Avenue
New York NY 10022
212-355-360

Reed Boyd
(74 above right, 144–45)
181–3 Kings Road
London SW3 5EB
England
(44) 171-351-1522

Luigi Roselli
(13 above, 21 below right,
36 left)
Surry Hills
2010 Sydney
New South Wales
Australia
(61) 2-9281-1498

Charles Rutherfoord
(23, 50 below right, 68–69, 74
below, 82, 128–29)
51 The Chase
London SW4 0NP
England
(44) 171-627-0182

Ash Sakula Architects
(28, 80 above, 156–57)
38 Mount Pleasant
London WC1X 0AN
England
(44) 171-837-9735

John F. Saladino
(83 above)
305 East 63rd Street
New York NY 10021
212-752-2440

Schack-Arnott
(149)
Danish Classic Moderne
Andrew Arnott & Karin Shack
517 High Street
Prahan
Victoria 3181
Australia
(61) 3-9525-0250

Emily Todhunter Interiors
(122, 124–25)
The Studio House
31 Kenley Walk
London W11 4XG
England
(44) 171-221-8006

Stephen Varady Architecture
(27 below, 56–57 below,
100 right)
Studio 5, 102 Albion Street
Surry Hills
2010 Sydney
Australia
(61) 2-9281-4825

Olivier Vidal Aia
(20, 65)
14 rue Moncey
75009 Paris
France
(33) 1 49.70.82.82

Vicente Wolfe Associates Inc
(66, 100 center, 129)
333 West 39th Street
New York NY 10018
212-465-0590

Woolf Architects
(17, 24, 70-71)
4th Floor Studios
39-51 Highgate Road
London NW5 1RT
England
(44) 171-428-9500

Index

Acknowledgements

The publisher thanks the photographers and organisations for their kind permission to reproduce the following photographs in this book:

1-2 Henry Bourne; **3** The Life Enhancing Tile Company; **4-5** Henry Bourne/Frédéric Méchiche's apartment in Paris; **6-7** Henry Bourne/a loft in London designed by Robert Dye Associates; **7 far left** Henry Bourne/rug by Garouste Bonnetti; **7 centre left** Henry Bourne/Roger Oates Design; **7 centre right** Henry Bourne; **7 far right** James Merrell; **8 above** Guy Bouchet; **8 below left** Henry Bourne/an apartment in London designed by Adjaye & Russell; **8 below right** Henry Bourne/an apartment in Paris designed by Olivier Vidal AIA; **8-9** Christian Sarramon; **9 above** Eric Morin; **9 below** Tim Goffe/Paxton Locher Architects; **10-11** Arcaid/Nicholas Kane/Architect Ken Rorrison; **11 left** Arcaid/Julie Phipps/designer Marilyn Phipps; **11 right** Henry Dourne/DAD Associates; **12 left** James Merrell/Robyn & Simon Carnachan's house in Adelaide; **12 above right** Undine Prohl/Ron Goldman, Malibu; **12 below right** Henry Bourne/Alan & Hepzibah's home in Sussex; **13 above** James Merrell/a house in Sydney designed by Luigi Rosselli; **13 below left** James Merrell/Andrew Parr's house in Melbourne; **13 below right** Henry Bourne/a mews house in London designed by Architects McDowell & Benedetti; **14** Henry Bourne/Alan & Hepzibah's home in Sussex; **14-15** Henry Bourne/Circus Architects; **15 left** Reiner Blunck; **15 above right** Elizabeth Whiting & Associates/Jean-Paul Bonhommet; **15 below right** Solvi Dos Santos/Mr & Mrs Patrick Frey's house in Paris; **16-17** Henry Bourne/Frédéric Méchiche's apartment in Paris; **17** Henry Bourne/a house in London designed by Woolf architects; **18 above left** Henry Bourne/a house in Devon designed by Anthony Hudson Architects; **18 above right** Elizabeth Whiting & Associates/Jean-Paul Bonhommet; **18 centre** Henry Bourne/an apartment in Paris designed by Mark Guard Architects; **18 below** The Interior Archive/Cecila Innes; **18-19** Henry Bourne/a loft in London designed by Robert Dye Associates; **20** Henry Bourne/an apartment in Paris designed by Olivier Vidal AIA; **21 above left** Henry Bourne/rug by Garouste Bonnetti; **21 below left** Henry Bourne/DAD Associates; **21 above right** Henry Bourne/Charles Rutherfoord's house in London; **21 centre right** Henry Bourne/a house in Devon designed by Anthony Hudson Architects; **21 below right** James Merrell/a house in Sydney designed by Luigi Rosselli; **22 above left** James Merrell/Interni Interior Design Consultancy; **22 above right** Agence Top/Pascal Chevalier/designer Christian Liaigre; **22 below left** Christian Sarramon; **22 below right** Henry Bourne/Felix Bonnier's apartment in Paris; **23** Henry Bourne/a house in London designed by Charles Rutherfoord; **24** Peter Cook/a house in London designed by Woolf architects; **25 above left** Henry Bourne/a house in London designed by Woolf architects; **25 above centre** Henry Bourne/Roger & Fay Oates' house in Herefordshire; **25 above right** Henry Bourne/Dan & Claire Thorne's town house in Dorset designed by Sarah Featherstone; **25 below left** Henry Bourne/a house in Devon designed by Anthony Hudson Architects; **25 below right** The Interior Archive/Fritz von der Schulenburg/designer John Stefanidis; **26 left** James Merrell; **26 right** Henry Bourne; **26-27** Henry Bourne/an apartment in London designed by Adjaye & Russell; **27 above** Reiner Blunck; **27 below** James Merrell/Amanda and Andrew Manning's apartment in Sydney designed by Stephen Varady Architecture; **28** Henry Bourne/an apartment in London designed by Ash Sakula Architects; **29 above left** Henry Bourne/Frédéric Méchiche's apartment in Paris; **29 centre left** James Merrell/a house in Sydney designed by Luigi Rosselli; **29 below left** Henry Bourne/an apartment in Paris designed by Mark Guard Architects; **29 right** Henry Bourne/Circus Architects; **30 above left** Henry Bourne/a house in Devon designed by Anthony Hudson Architects; **30 above right** Henry Bourne; **30 below left** Henry Bourne/a house in London designed by Charles Rutherfoord; **30 below right** Henry Bourne/Circus Architects; **30-31** Paul Ryan/International Interiors/Kriistina Ratia; **31** Henry Bourne/design Charles Rutherfoord; **32-33** Henry Bourne/an apartment in Paris designed by Mark Guard Architects; **33** Henry Bourne; **34 above left** Dominique Vorillon; **34 above centre**, above right & below right Henry Bourne; **34 below left** & below centre James Merrell; **34-35** James Merrell/Hilton McConnico's house near Paris; **35 above left & below right** James Merrell; **35 above right & below left** Henry Bourne; **36 left** James Merrell/a house in Sydney designed by Luigi Rosselli; **36 centre** Guy Bouchet; **36 right** David Phelps/ designer Pat Guthman; **37** James Merrell/Khai Liew & Sue Kellet's house in Adelaide; **38** Guy Bouchet; **38-39** The Interior Archive/Simon Brown/designer John Stefanidis; **40 left** Henry Bourne/Frédéric Méchiche's apartment in Paris; **40 centre** James Merrell/François Gilles & Dominique Lubar, IPL Interiors; **40 right** The Interior Archive/Johnathon Pilkington/interior designer Lucy Ward; **41** Henry Bourne/Frédéric Méchiche's apartment in Paris; **42-43** Henry Bourne/a house in Devon designed by Anthony Hudson Architects; **43** Henry Bourne/Dan & Claire Thorne's town house designed by Sarah Featherstone; **44 above left** Arcaid/Simon Kelly/Belle/Architects P Stronach & T Allison, Sydney; **44 above centre** James Merrell/François Gilles & Dominique Lubar, IPL Interiors; **44 above right** Henry Bourne/a house in Devon designed by Anthony Hudson Architects; **45 above left** James Merrell/a house in London designed by François Gilles & Dominique Lubar, IPL Interiors; **45 above centre** Deidi von Schaewen/Architect Marc Korbiase; **45 above right** Jean-Pierre Godeau; **46-47** Henry Bourne/a house in Devon designed by Anthony Hudson Architects; **48 left** James Merrell/François Gilles & Dominique Lubar, IPL Interiors; **48 centre** Henry Bourne/a loft in London designed by Robert Dye Associates; **48 right** Henry Bourne/Linda Trahair's house in Bath; **49** James Merrell/an apartment in New York designed by Campion A Platt Architect; **50 left** Paul Ryan/International Interiors/designer Kaffe Fassett; **50 right** Henry Bourne/a house in London designed by Charles Rutherfoord; **50-51** James Merrell/a terrace in London designed by Christophe Gollut; **51 above** The Interior Archive/Fritz von der Schulenburg; **51 centre** James Merrell /Khai Liew & Sue Kellett; **51 below** James Merrell/an apartment in New York designed by Pentagram; **52-53** James Merrell/Frédéric Méchiche's house near Toulon; **53 left** James Merrell/ Frédéric Méchiche's house near Toulon; **53 right** Christian Sarramon/Terence Conran, Provence; **54 left** Henry Bourne/Roger Oates Design; **54 centre** Elizabeth Whiting & Associates/Jean-Paul Bonhommet; **54 right** Yves Duronsoy/Christine & Michel Gerard at Le Couvent aux Herbes, Eugenie-les-Bains; **55** James Merrell/Khai Liew & Sue Kellett's house in Adelaide; **56** James Merrell/a house in Sydney designed by Interni Interior Design Consultancy; **56-57 above** James Merrell/a house in Sydney designed by Interni Interior Design Consultancy; **56-57 below** James Merrell/ Linda Parham and David Slobam's apartment designed by Stephen Varady Architecture; **57 above left** Henry Bourne/Alan and Hepzibah's home in Sussex; **57 above right** James Merrell/Amanda and Andrew Manning's apartment in Sydney designed by Stephen Varady Architecture; **57 below** James Merrell/Interni Interior Design Consultancy; **58 left** Henry Bourne; **58 centre** The Life Enhancing Tile Company; **58 right** Christian Sarramon; **58-59** Reiner Blunck/Architect Johannes Manderscheid, Rottenburg; **59 left** Christian Sarramon; **59 above right** interior designer Denis Colomb; **59 below right** James Merrell; **60 left** Deidi von Schaewen/Architects Donati-Dubors; **60 centre** Antonio Martinelli/Architect Christopher Stead; **60 right** Erica Lennard (Nilaya Hermitage Hotel, Goa India); **61** Henry Bourne/a mews house in London designed by McDowell & Benedetti; **62** Reiner Blunck; **62-63** Henry Bourne/a loft in London designed by DAD Associates; **63 left** Henry Bourne/a loft in London designed by DAD Associates; **63 right** James Merrell/Amy & Richard Sachs' apartment in New York designed by Vicente Wolfe; **64 above left** Erica Lennard (La Chabaude, Apt, France); **64 above centre** Marie Claire Maison/Gilles de Chabaneix/Catherine de Puech; **64 above right** Erica Lennard (apartment of Erica Lennard, designer Roberto Bergero); **64 below left** Guy Bouchet; **64 below right** Jean-Pierre Godeau; **64-65** Henry Bourne/an apartment in Paris designed by Olivier Vidal AIA; **66** James Merrell/Vicente Wolfe's apartment in New York; **67** Henry Bourne/Felix Bonnier's apartment in New York; **68 left** Henry Bourne/a house in London designed by Woolf architects; **68 right** Henry Bourne/a house in London designed by Mark Guard Architects; **68-69** Hcnry Dourne/Charles Rutherfoord's house in London; **69 above** Henry Bourne/Charles Rutherfoord's house in London; **69 below** Henry Bourne/a mews house in London designed by Architect McDowell & Benedetti; **70-71** Henry Bourne/a house in London designed by Woolf architects; **71 far left** David George; **71 centre left & far right** Henry Bourne; **71 centre right** James Merrell; **72 left** Antonio Martinelli/Architect John Pawson; **72 below right** Henry Bourne/a loft in London designed by Robert Dye Associates; **72-73** Henry Bourne/ Frédéric Méchiche's apartment in Paris; **73 above left** Marie Claire Maison/Francis Amiand/Julie Borgeaud; **73 above right** James Merrell/an apartment in London designed by Charles Rutherfoord; **73 below left** Henry Bourne/Charles Rutherfoord's house in London; **74 above left** James Merrell; **74 above centre** Henry Bourne; **74 above right** James Merrell/Keith Varty and Alan Cleaver's apartment in London designed by Reed & Boyd; **74 below** Henry Bourne/a house in London designed by Charles Rutherfoord; **75 above left** Christian Sarramon; **75 above right** Dominique Vorillon/Architects

Angelil/Coraham; **75 below left** Paul Ryan/International Interiors; **75 below right** Simon Brown; **76 above left** James Merrell/an apartment in New York designed by Pentagram; **76 above right** James Merrell/Andrew Parr's house in Melbourne; **76 below left** James Merrell/a house in Sydney designed by Interni Interior Design Consultancy; **76 below centre** James Merrell/a house in Noosaville designed by John Mainwaring; **76 below right** James Merrell/Interni Interior Design Consultancy; **77** Henry Bourne/Felix Bonnier's apartment in Paris; **78 above** James Merrell/Andrew Parr's house in Melbourne; **78 centre** Henry Bourne/a house in Devon designed by Anthony Hudson Architects; **78 below** James Merrell/Nicholas Larcombe and Caroline Solomon's house in Sydney; **78-79** Henry Bourne/a house in Devon designed by Anthony Hudson Architects; **81 above** Henry Bourne/an apartment in London designed by Ash Sakula Architects; **81 below left** Henry Bourne; 81 **below centre** Henry Bourne/a house in London designed by Charles Rutherfoord; **81 below right** Henry Bourne/DAD Associates; **82** Henry Bourne/a house in London designed by Charles Rutherfoord; **83 above** James Merrell/John F. Saladino's apartment in New York; **83 centre** Elizabeth Whiting & Associates/Michael Dunne/designers Juan Molyneux, Andrée Putnam, Linda Macklowe, Todd Williams; **83 below** James Merrell; **84** James Merrell/a house in London designed by Charles Rutherfoord; **84-85** Tim Goffe /Paxton Locher Architects; **85** Arcaid/John Edward Linden/Nick Butcher & Christian Davies; **86 above left** Arcaid/Jeremy Cockayne; **86 above right** Deidi von Schaewen/designer Craig Port; **86 centre** James Merrell/ Vincent Dané's house near Biarritz; **86 below** Paul Ryan/International Interiors/M Kreigel; **87** Henry Bourne/ Frédéric Méchiche's apartment in Paris; **88** Henry Bourne/Amanda Freedman's house in London; **89 above left** The Interior Archive/Henry Wilson; **89 above centre & below left** Henry Bourne/Amanda Freedman's house in London; **89 above right** Henry Bourne/a loft in London designed by DAD Associates; **89 below right** Henry Bourne/a house in London designed by Mark Guard Architects; **90 above** Marie Claire Maison/Gilles de Chabaneix/Marie Kalt; **90 below left** James Merrell/an apartment in New York designed by Jacqueline Coumans, Le Decor Français with the help of Olivier Gelbsmann; **90-91** Arcaid/Alberto Piovanno/architect Mario Boggia; **91** James Merrell/designer Charlotte Barnes; **92 left** Henry Bourne; **92 centre** Christian Sarramon; **92 right** Undine Pröhl/Architect Natalye Appex, Texas; **93** James Merrell/François Gilles & Dominique Lubar, IPL Interiors; **94** James Merrell; **94-95** The Interior Archive/Christopher Simon Sykes/designer Celia Lyttletton; **96 above left** James Merrell/Diane Atkinson & Patrick Hughes' loft in London designed by Michael Green of Green Homan; **96 above right** Solvi Dos Santos; **96 centre** James Merrell/Sue and Andy's apartment in Blackheath; **96-97** The Interior Archive/Henry Wilson; **97 left** The Interior Archive/Ari Ashley; **97 right** Arcaid/Ken Kirkwood/designer Lyn le Grice; **98 above** Paul Ryan/International Interiors/designer Lyn le Grice; **98 below** David Phelps/designer Karen Linder; **98-99 above** Paul Ryan/International Interiors/designer Lyn le Grice; **98-99 below** Michael Garland; **99 above** David George; **99 below** The Interior Archive/Simon Upton; **100 left** James Merrell/Christophe Gollut's apartment in London; **100 centre** James Merrell/Shelly Washington's apartment in New York designed by Vicente Wolfe; **100 right** James Merrell/Linda Parham and David Slobam's apartment in Melbourne designed by Stephen Varady architecture; **101** Henry Bourne/Felix Bonnier's apartment in Paris; **102-103** Henry Bourne/Richard Mabb & Kate Green's apartment in London; **103 far left & far right** Henry Bourne; **103 centre left** Henry Bourne/Sinclair-Till; **103 centre right** James Merrell; **104-105** Marianne Majerus/designer Mary Rose Young; **106** Tim Street-Porter/designer Daniel Sacks; **107 left** Camera Press; **107 right** The Interior Archive/Johnathan Pilkington; **108 left** Henry Bourne/Richard Mabb and Kate Green's apartment in London; **108-109** Henry Bourne/an apartment in London designed by Robert Dye Associates; **109** Henry Bourne/Dan and Claire Thorne's town house in Dorset designed by Sarah Featherstone; **110** Paul Ryan/International Interiors/Stamberg Aferiat Architects; **111 above** Reiner Blunck; **111 below** Henry Bourne/floor by Dalsouple, First Floor; **112** James Merrell/Sue and Andy's apartment in Blackheath; **112-113** The Interior Archive/James Mortimer; **113** Henry Bourne/John Raab's apartment in London/floor by Sinclair Till; **114** Ray Main; **115** Henry Bourne/ Ellen O'Neill; **116 above** Arcaid/Ray Main/Rhode design; **116 below left** The Interior Archive/James Mortimer/Michael Howells; **116 below right** Tim Street-Porter/designer Cedric Gibbons; **116-117** The Interior Archive/Simon Brown/Polly Dickens; **118 above left** David Phelps; **118 above right** Arcaid/Ken Kirkwood; **118 below left** David Phelps/courtesy American Homestyle; **118**

below right Eric Morin; **119** Henry Bourne/Circus Architects/floor by First Floor; **120** The Interior Archive/Jonathan Pilkington; **121 left** Elizabeth Whiting & Associates/Rodney Hyett; **121 right** David Phelps/courtesty of American Homestyle; **122** Henry Bourne/an apartment in London designed by Emily Todhunter; **123 left** Henry Bourne/a house in London designed by Charles Rutherfoord; **123 above right** Paul Ryan/International Interiors/Corinne Calessa; **123 below right** The Interior Archive/Tim Beddow; **124-125** Henry Bourne/an apartment in London designed by Emily Todhunter/rug by Garouste & Bonnetti; **125 left & right** Henry Bourne; **125 far left & far right** Henry Bourne/Roger Oates Design; **126 left** Eric Morin; **126 right** James Merrell/rug by Woodnotes; **127 left** James Merrell; **127 above right** James Merrell/Sarah Elson's house in London/rug by June Hilton; **127 below right** Henry Bourne/Roger Oates Design; **128 left** James Merrell/an apartment in London designed by François Gilles & Dominique Lubar; **128 centre** Henry Bourne/an apartment in London designed by Emily Todhunter; **128 right** James Merrell; **128-129** Henry Bourne/a house in London designed by Charles Rutherfoord; **129** James Merrell/Shelly Washington's apartment in New York designed by Vicente Wolfe; **130 left** Henry Bourne/an apartment in London designed by Ash Sakula Architects; **130 above right** James Merrell; **130 below right** Henry Bourne/a mews house in London designed by McDowell & Benedetti; **130-131** Henry Bourne/a mews house in London designed by McDowell & Benedetti; **132-133** Henry Bourne/Amanda Freedman's house in London; **134 left** Christian Sarramon/Claire Bataille; **134 right** Henry Bourne/floor by Helen Yardley; **135** Henry Bourne/floor by Helen Yardley; **136** Elizabeth Whiting & Associates/Andreas von Einsiedel/designer Chester Jones; **136-137** Henry Bourne/Dan and Claire Thorne's town house designed by Claire Featherstone; **137** Eric Morin; **138-139** Henry Bourne/ Frédéric Méchiche's apartment in Paris; **139 above** Paul Ryan/International Interiors/Katherine Fortescue; **139 below** James Merrell/Andrew Parr's house in Melbourne; **140** Henry Bourne/Roger & Fay Oates' house in Herefordshire; **141 above right** Henry Bourne/Frédéric Méchiche's apartment in Paris; **141 below left** Agence Top/Pascal Chevalier/designer Hubert de Givenchy; **141 below centre** David Phelps/courtesy of American Homestyle; **141 below right** Richard Davies; **142 above** Paul Ryan/International Interiors/Fell-Clark Design; **142 below left** Eric Morin; **142 below centre** Christian Sarramon; **142 below right** The Interior Archive/Henry Wilson; **143** Henry Bourne/Linda Trahair's house in Bath; **144 above** Dominique Vorillon/Angelil/Graham Architects; **144 below** James Merrell; **144-145** Simon Upton/Ann Boyd's apartment in London; **145 above** Henry Bourne/Felix Bonnier's apartment in Paris; **145 below** James Merrell/a house in London designed by François Gilles & Dominique Lubar, IPL Interiors; **146** Arcaid/Richard Bryant/The Mount Vernon Ladies Association of the Union; **146-147** The Interior Archive/Henry Wilson/designer Christopher Davies; **147 above left** Henry Bourne; **147 below left** Henry Bourne/Charles Rutherfoord's house in London; **147 right** Henry Bourne/Roger & Fay Oates' house in Herefordshire; **148 left** James Merrell; **148 right** Elizabeth Whiting & Associates/Rodney Hyett; **149** James Merrell/rug by Woodnotes; **150 left** James Merrell; **150 right** Elizabeth Whiting & Associates/Rodney Hyett; **151 left** Henry Bourne; **151 right** The Interior Archive/Fritz von der Schulenburg/Emily Todhunter; **152 left** Christian Sarramon; **152 centre** James Merrell; **152 right** James Merrell/an apartment in London designed by François Gilles & Dominique Lubar, IPL Interiors; **153 above** James Merrell/an apartment in New York designed by Jacqueline Coumans, Le Decor Français with the help of Oliver Gelbsmann; **153 below left** Elizabeth Whiting & Associates/Andreas von Einsiedel; **153 below right** The Interior Archive/Peter Woloszynski; **154** Henry Bourne/Roger & Fay Oates' house in Herefordshire; **154-155** Henry Bourne/Roger & Fay Oates' house in Herefordshire; **155 above** Henry Bourne/Roger & Fay Oates' house in Herefordshire; **155 below left** Henry Bourne/Roger & Fay Oates' house in Herefordshire; **155 below right** James Merrell/a house in London designed by François Gilles & Dominique Lubar, IPL Interiors; **156** James Merrell/rug designed by Christine Vanderhurd; **156-157** Henry Bourne/an apartment in London designed by Ash Sakula Architects/rug by Christopher Farr; **157 above** Henry Bourne/rug by Christopher Farr; **157 below** James Merrell/Sarah Elson's house in London/rug by Christopher Farr; **158 above** Henry Bourne/Alan & Hepzibah's home in Sussex/rug by Annette Nix; **158 below** Marco Ricca/rug by Christine Vanderhurd; **158-159** Marco Ricca/rug by Christine Vanderhurd; **159** Henry Bourne/Alan & Hepzibah's home in Sussex/rug by Annette Nix; **160** James Merrell/Interni Interior Design Consultancy; **161 far left & far right** Henry Bourne; **161 centre** James Merrell.

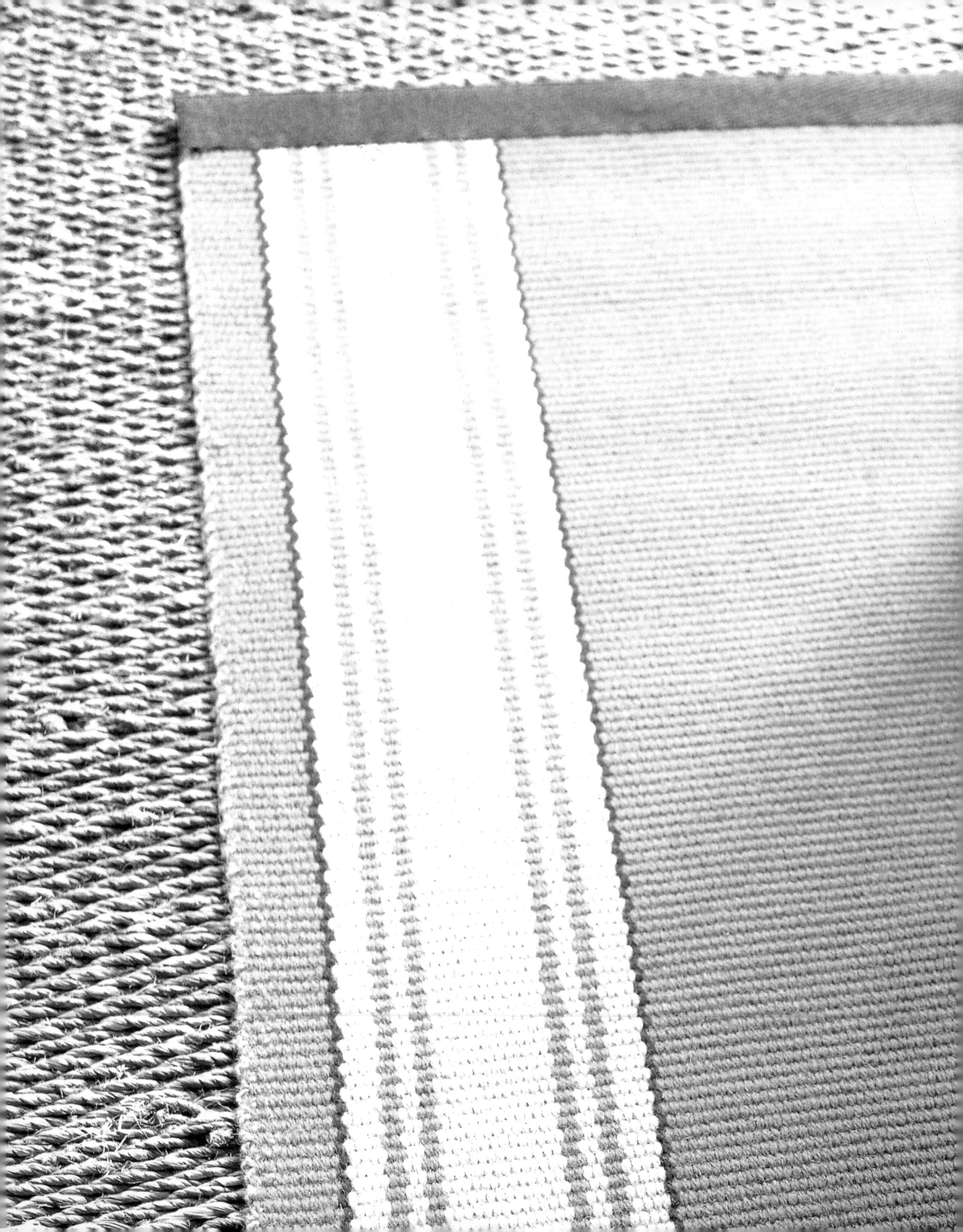